Cyber Fraud:

The Web of Lies

US MARINE RISKS LIFE IN PRISON

TO EXPOSE A CYBERCRIME

THAT CONSUMERS KNOW NOTHING ABOUT.

Bryan Seely

Cyber Fraud: The Web of Lies

Published by
Seely Security
An XSIVE1 Company

ISBN: 978-1-533-15677-8

For Aurora, Piper & Declan.

Table of Contents

One

Uncovering the Scam

"I just replaced all the locks on a client's house. They had called a locksmith that they found on Google Maps to put in an electronic pin code deadbolt on their house. Three weeks later, their house was robbed. When they looked for the locksmith on Google Maps, the business was no longer there."

-Seattle locksmith, June 2015

Chances are that if you are reading this book (or are otherwise alive in 2016 or beyond), you have used the Internet for a while. You have an email account that you check regularly, use your smart phones to shop for pizza, clothing, appliances, or maybe even your next date. The Internet has made the world of commerce, social interaction, and entertainment much more available to everyone.

The Internet has also made it much easier for criminals to get access to the general public. Just like your grandma, they are gradually becoming more technologically savvy. And just like with grandma, this development has frightening implications. Unfortunately for the general public, technology has also made it much harder to track criminals, as the trail of evidence is no longer hairs and fibers from clothing, but digital records that are often faked or deleted.

The Internet is also no longer confined to desktop computers. We have tablets, smart phones, and laptops that access the Internet from nearly anywhere. It's become so commonplace that the very notion of being somewhere without Internet access strikes us as an unthinkable hardship. This increased Internet availability has made it even easier for people to become the victims of cyber fraud.

Most of us are well aware of the typical scams that are associated with the Internet. I can tell you that the first time that I received an email from a Nigerian prince with a banking conundrum, I was extremely excited at the possibility of a 10 million dollar cash payday for assisting him. Needless to say, ultimately both of us were disappointed. Because I did not have any money to give him to help release the funds, I could only email him back and wish him the best of luck in his pursuit for justice. This is known as a 419 scam.

419 scams are a type of fraud and one of the most common types of confidence trick. The scam typically involves promising the victim a significant share of a large sum of money, which the fraudster requires a small up-front payment to obtain. If a victim makes the payment, the fraudster either invents a series of further fees for the victim, or simply disappears.

There are many variations on this type of scam, including advance-fee fraud, Fifo's Fraud, Spanish Prisoner Scam, the black money scam, and the Detroit-Buffalo scam. The number "419" refers to the article of the Nigerian Criminal Code dealing with fraud. The scam has been used with fax and traditional mail, and is now used with the Internet.

Online versions of the scam originate primarily in the United States, the United Kingdom and Nigeria, with Ivory Coast, Togo, South Africa, the Netherlands, and Spain also having high incidences of such fraud.[i]

Most of us get emails like this all the time. Nearly every email provider is aware of these types of scams, so they automatically filter and remove them so you don't accidently click on a malicious attachment.

Funny note: I received a piece of spam email while typing this chapter that managed to get through my spam filters. Most of the message is in the subject line, with little or nothing in the body of the email.

Subject:
"Greetings to you, I'M LIEUTENANT GENERAL SUSAN, I am a UNITED STATE ARMY GENERAL, From united state of America, i want you to contact me so i will send you my pictures"

Wow. A 3-star general who misspelled "United States", apparently likes to shout (all caps on the Internet means shouting) and does not use proper capitalization when not shouting. And instead of offering me influence over military policy, she's offering me that rarest of commodities on the Internet; pictures of a woman.

There are many other ways that scammers target the public. In addition to Nigerian princes who need help from random strangers, there are many other types of fraud that occur on the Internet on a daily basis.

- Ponzi Schemes & Investment Fraud
- Identity Theft
- Email Phishing
- Ransomware
- Spam Email

All online fraud shares one common goal. That is to get access to someone else's money, i.e., your money, your company's money, or anyone else's money. It doesn't really matter whose, and there are thousands of ways to accomplish their goal. Criminals use the Internet, phone, postal mail, and anything else they think may help them get someone else's money. They are persistent because it has worked before, and chances are that it will work again.

I don't want to sound like I am sympathetic to the scammers by saying that I understand why they choose this path. Many of them come from bad upbringings, poor countries, or other economic situations that don't give them a lot of options for success. But that doesn't mean that they are justified in hopping on the Internet and trying to scam anyone they possibly can so they can strike it rich.

There have been many reported[1] instances of people falling victim to scammers overseas pretending to be someone they are not.

- A woman named Sarah met a man named "Chris Olsen" online who was a businessman working in Africa. She sent him $1.4 million without ever meeting him.[ii]
- Janella Spears of Oregon sent $400,000 to Nigerian con artists, believing she would be made rich by helping them. The whole thing started with a request for $100, and built up from there.[iii]
- Pam Krause of Almond, Wis., thought she was helping out a desperate mother in West Africa. Instead, she lost $18,000 to an elaborate, high-tech swindle, one of the many variations of the so-called "Nigerian scams."[iv]
- A man in San Antonio was arrest in 2014 for assisting Nigerian scammers by receiving money from victims and sending a portion back to Nigeria.[v]

It would be criminal (pardon the pun) to talk about modern scams without mentioning Bernie Madoff. He was a very successful American businessman, stockbroker, investment banker and even the former non-executive chairman of the NASDAQ stock exchange. It sounds like that guy had a lot going for him.

---

[1] Remember: just because something is published on the Internet doesn't mean that it's accurate. See, you know, this entire book.

In December of 2008, he was arrested for securities fraud.[vi] It turns out that his very successful asset management firm was a giant Ponzi scheme. In fact, he transformed a legitimate company that he founded in 1960 into the largest known Ponzi scheme in history. According to federal investigators, the losses to clients total 65 billion dollars. Mr. Madoff "made-off"[2] with quite a lot of money.

Madoff was sentenced to the maximum amount of time in prison for his crimes, which is 150 years. I would think that they could have just said "life plus 1 day", or 150,000 years. It wouldn't really make a difference if it were 149 years or 151 years. 150 years seems very arbitrary, albeit effective.

Though when geneticists find a way to extend human life by 50-100 years, there are going to be a lot of politicians and lawmakers with egg on their faces when they have to release prisoners from jail after their 150 year sentences are complete (not that politicians don't already have enough egg on their faces from their own shenanigans).[3]

As you can see by some of these examples, scammers don't always come from poor African nations. They can be men, women, African, American, white, black, Asian, young or old. People who make a living by scamming others cannot be easily identified. So when

---

[2] See? Punny

[3] I would give you a list of recent political blunders, but this book was written during the presidential campaign of Donald Trump, which renders the list too long and elastic to even try to encapsulate. Yes, future generations, Donald Trump once ran for president.

trying to find them, it is both unfair and unhelpful to profile people by race, ethnicity, or gender. Perhaps somewhere, right now, an actual Nigerian prince is in need of legitimate assistance (but probably not, because Nigeria abolished its monarchy in 1963).

Some of the stories I just mentioned happened very recently, which means that not everyone using the Internet is aware of these common types of online fraud. Criminals are still sending the emails and still managing to find victims, even when their scamming methods are so well known, because the payoff is huge. The risk of them getting caught and prosecuted is also very low, so for them, it is a risk well worth taking.

There are, however, scams that are far less known; some of which started well before the invention of the Internet. What we know as the Internet became publicly available in the 1990's, but that does not mean that people suddenly became criminals to take advantage of the newly available World Wide Web. The expression "There's a sucker born every minute and two to take him." is older than the airplane. Scamming is an old profession. Stopping fraud is one of the most important duties of government, and has been for a long time.

Before the Internet, you had to rely on an archaic tome called "the Yellow Pages" in order to find business information. This giant book, which magically[4] appeared on your doorstep, contained page

---

[4] The Yellow Pages was delivered by people. There's no such thing as magic.

after yellow page of categorized businesses, sorted alphabetically. If you needed to call a plumber or a lawyer, you would "let your fingers do the walking."

Most people are probably unaware that criminals and scammers found a way to manipulate the Yellow Pages directory. (Yes, people even found ways to hack books!) Every category inside the Yellow Pages was sorted alphabetically, as it was the easiest way to look up a business by name. The problem with printed materials is that they are not able to be resorted or changed after printing, which is why after the invention of the Internet, the Yellow Pages books are now more commonly used to line birdcages than to find your local pizza parlor.

Scammers found that if they named their companies something starting with the letter "A", it would be at the front of the business category, and therefore get more visibility from consumers.

Consumers who need an attorney, plumber, or carpet cleaner, are not going to call 20 different places and get quotes. With no websites or information other than the business name, they are probably going to call one or two places near the beginning of the list to purchase the service they need.

Also, before the invention of the Internet, there was a telephone service called 411. 411 goes back as far as 1930 in New York City and San Francisco and has been a very useful tool for consumers to find local business information.[vii]

Since I have included it in this book, you've probably guessed that the 411 directory was somehow used by scammers. You're right. Scammers found a way to get fake business listings into the database of local businesses that directory assistance provided to consumers. I know that it would be hard to imagine why someone would do this, but remember, this is the beginning of the book.

Same Old Scam

The phone book and 411 directory assistance were made obsolete by the Internet, and even the Internet has changed quite a bit in the last 20 years. People don't just sit at their computers anymore; they are often searching and finding information on their mobile phones while on the train, or sitting at a coffee shop. One reason that members of the general public are often referred to as "consumers" is because they "consume" things. Consumers are typically pictured on days like Black Friday and other high shopping days rushing into stores (and even trampling on the weaker of their fellow consumers) to purchase televisions, clothing or other consumable goods.

Besides consumables, consumers have a need for services, which are typically home, business, or automotive services. Here are some common services that the typical homeowner would use.

- Locksmiths
- Plumbers
- Electricians
- Carpet Cleaners

- General Contractors

The people who gamed the system with the Yellow Pages and 411 moved onto the Internet as consumers shifted from looking at the phone book to the variety of directory websites that now exist.

You might be wondering why people would put fake businesses online, and how could they possibly be "scamming" or committing fraud. Well, you are not alone, as it is one of the most common questions I have had when talking about this subject since I first got involved.

In order for me to talk about these things in more detail, we are going to have to define what we are talking about.

Local Business Directory: This is a website that provides users relevant information about local businesses. You search for a pizza place, and the website provides you a pizza place; typically on a map, and helps you with directions, hours of operation, pictures, reviews or other relevant information. Examples of this are: Google Places, Apple Maps, Yelp.com, Yahoo Local, WhitePages.com, and Angie's List.

Business Listing: This refers to one record, meaning one specific business. This would contain the Business Name, Address, Phone Number. Often times it will have the company website, hours, or other information about the company.

To give you an example of how I will use this term: I created a business listing for my company on Yelp.com. Meaning, I entered in my business details on Yelp.com so that Yelp would show my business on its website and mobile app.

Fictitious Business Listing: Same thing as a Business Listing, but the information is not real; it is made up and used to scam or defraud users.

Here are three hypothetical scenarios that will help you understand how this fraud can occur and what it typically looks like.

Scenario 1

Joe Frauderson[5] has a pool company in Irvine, California. He has his business listed on Google Maps, Yahoo, Bing and Yelp.

He wants to expand his company, but opening a second physical store costs money in rent, staff, advertising and other expenses. It might ultimately become profitable, but it's a huge risk. If it fails, he could go bankrupt. So he creates a fictitious business listing in Los Angeles on Google My Business, Bing, Yahoo and other sites. This could get him a lot of business in the Los Angeles area. Calls begin to come to the new phone number for his fake business listing, and Joe starts to get clients in the Los Angeles area without having to spend a dime on marketing, advertising, or opening a new store.

---

[5] This name of this hypothetical scammer was selected and intended to be humorous and obviously fictitious. No offense or defamation is intended to any decent and honorable bearers of the Frauderson name.

Scenario 2

Joe decides that after creating 30 fake pool cleaning business listings that he doesn't actually want to clean pools anymore. Cleaning pools is a lot of work, and the calls keep coming from all over Los Angeles County and Orange County. Joe decides to sell the phone calls he receives to other companies and charge them for every referral.

These calls are called "leads".[6] Since each call can result in a pretty decent monthly contract, each call could be worth $40-50 each. Typical pool service can cost $100 a month, and that's $1200 a year. For most companies, finding clients is the hard part, and Joe has that problem solved.

Joe begins forwarding all the individual phone numbers for each fake business listing to other pool companies. At the end of every month, Joe sends them an invoice for $50 per call, multiplied by the number of calls that he sent them.

The pool companies are happy to receive the "referrals" and pay him for the calls. Joe now doesn't have to clean pools.

As you can see in these two scenarios, the consumers who ends up calling the fake business listing don't have any clue that they are calling a fake business.

---

[6]To learn more about "leads", as well as to see one of the finest monologues in American cinema and where Frank Underwood worked before "House of Cards", see "Glengarry Glen Ross".

Think about this for a second.

You call **First Search Results Pool Cleaning** from a search on Bing.

The person who answers the phone says:

"Pool cleaners, how may I help you?"

You wanted a pool cleaner and you got a pool cleaner.

After they come by and clean your pool, you pay them.

Let's take a look at alternatives to the above scenario.

Scenario 3

It's the same Joe from Scenario 1, except now he has no business license, no bonding, and no insurance. He overcharges customers, works fast and sloppy, and causes damage at customer homes and businesses. You want to report Joe to the better business bureau. You file a complaint with the local police.

But the problem here is that they can't find Joe. You try to show the cops the business listing for his company and it's gone. The phone number no longer works and he has removed the business listing. He is gone without a trace. All Joe has to do now is change the business name and start over again.

What if Joe were to damage your home? How could you file an insurance claim against him? How could you take him to court?

Come to think of it, "Joe Frauderson" might not have even been his real name. Joe could be a registered sex offender, convicted felon,

Sagittarius[7], or any number of awful things. This is not the type of person you would want coming in your home to do repairs, or spending time around you and your family.

These are not crazy hypothetical scenarios. They are actual situations that occur every single day, in every city in the United States. It isn't an unknown problem either; it's just hard to summarize or identify the people behind it and every story is slightly different. It is hard to see behind the curtain and identify which listings are real and fake, especially if you are not aware that listings CAN be faked.

Most people have no clue that is even a possibility. Consumer protection is a very high priority with respect to most forms of communication, and it simply does not register with the vast majority of the public that a source of information as ubiquitous as the Internet could be safe haven for frauds and cheats. As you can see, it takes time just to lay out the problem clearly.

These scenarios go back to the days of the phone book, and 411 directory assistance era as well. Many scams of this kind started well before the invention of the Internet.

The businesses that are typically faked are service-based businesses that serve customers at the customer location, rather than at a brick and mortar location. Think about it: when was the last time you

---

[7]This is obviously meant as a joke. Everybody knows that all frauds are Scorpios.

went to your landscaper's office, or your plumber's office? Those types of companies usually don't get customers at their offices.

Here is a list of business types that are plagued with fake online businesses.

- Air conditioning repair/installation
- Appliance Repair
- Auto glass repair and installation
- Bail bonds
- Carpet cleaners/installers
- Commercial chimney sweeping
- Commercial office cleaning
- Drug rehab counseling
- Duct cleaning
- Electrician
- Garage door repair/installations
- General contractors
- Handyman
- Home security installations
- HVAC contractors
- Landscapers
- Lawyers
- Locksmiths
- Mobile auto repair
- Mobile detailing
- Movers
- Party rentals, DJs, and bounce houses
- Pest Control

- Pool Cleaning
- Plumbing
- Pool cleaners
- Residential home painting

These businesses are designed to serve customers at the customer's location and never at the corporate office. Indeed, a lot of these businesses are run out of people's homes. Most of these businesses are perfectly legitimate, but there are those that are not. And when the customer can't visit the business's physical location, the situation is ripe for scammers to set up fake businesses.

There are a lot of business directory websites that provide this type of data. The site with the most users is Google Maps, followed by Apple Maps and Bing, Yelp, and many others after that.

According a digital research company named ComScore, Google Maps is the most popular local business directory app.[viii]

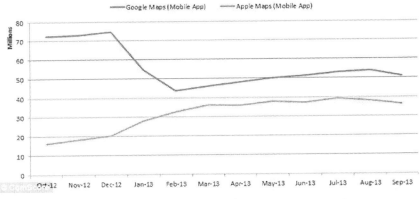

Figure 1.1[ix]

That does not include users who use Google's desktop search to locate relevant business data. Until recently, Apple Maps was not previously available via a desktop browser, but that has changed with some of the recent OSX versions. However, Google continues to dominate the local business directories online for desktop and mobile app searches.

Here is a short list of companies that also provide local business data for consumers.

- Google
- Bing
- Yahoo!
- Yelp
- Angie's List
- Whitepages
- SuperPages

The clear leader in the mapping and local business directories is Google Maps and its "My Business" product. Apple Maps provides some level of competition in the mapping and search realms, particularly because of the popularity of the iPhone and because the application comes with all new iPhones. This is overshadowed by the fact that the Google Maps app is available on both iPhone and Android devices, and Android has been dominating the mobile device war in the US and abroad for a while now. Google wanted to be the best at many different things, and it has absolutely accomplished that goal.

To give you an idea of how well Apple and Google are doing, the International Business Times reported that Google is worth $364.99 Billion and Apple is worth a staggering $598.73 Billion. In the same article it is reported that Google will have no trouble beating Apple in the race to being valued at $1 Trillion, and the first company on Earth to do so.

Google has done very well at becoming the best; it has also painted a large target on its back for hackers and criminals seeking to exploit Google's success. Google's search engine is the default for most people, and its name has become synonymous with any online searching.

As the general public defaults to Google for web searches, local business searches, video searches, news and other content, criminals are right behind. As mentioned earlier, criminals are already a daily reality with their email spamming, and what I am here to tell you is that they have become so entrenched into the Internet search ecosystem that has been a nightmare for many people.

I will be going into a lot of detail throughout this book about the various problems with not only Google Maps, but other directories as well. You will see technical comparisons, examples, screenshots, and even evidence and in depth looks at the spammers that exist on all of the current search engines.

Personally, I love and use many of the products that Google has created, and think that the company as a whole does a lot of amazing things. It is often the leader in new software and other technology software, providing many free services and products to the online community, and this book is not one man's crusade against some goliath that needs to be stopped. There are plenty of companies worldwide that may deserve public shaming, but I personally do not think that Google is among them. I just firmly believe that it needs to change how it operates and improve the lives of millions of their customers. And perhaps, in so doing, make even more money.

That being said, when I started to get involved about a year and a half ago, I quickly concluded that things in the Google Maps world were not adding up. Part of the problem is that the entire problem is hard to describe clearly. The public isn't familiar with the types of scams and fraud that are going on, so it becomes a very difficult sell to the media. The media has reported various problems and stories over the past few years related to maps fraud; yet the problems persist.

- Schneier on Security   - March 2009
  Google Maps Spam[x]

- NBCNews.com   - July 2007
  Locked out? Don't fall for this locksmith scam[xi]

- The Guardian   - July 2014
  Restaurant owner sues Google over Maps listing 'sabotage[xii]

These reported victims are people like you who have called a fake business and had problems like I have already described. They call the police, leave bad reviews, but nothing seems to change. The only place that some of these criminals may exist is on Google Maps, or at least that is where they start. The criminals don't target Bing alone, or Whitepages.com, or any other directory because the payoff is too small to make it worthwhile.

When you can manipulate the results on Google Maps, you can earn a king's ransom. How do I know?

Well, later on I will show you secret documents of an ~~actual~~ pretend[8] spamming organization, including how many calls they receive, the

---

[8]My legal counsel told me to make sure that I clarify that this is a "pretend"

type of income that earn, invoices, as well as identify many fake listings that just might still be online right this very second.

You can go look for them yourself. I don't want to spoil the surprise, but these types of organizations are very good at tricking the public; even posting fake reviews by the thousands that are still online to this day.

Consumers aren't the only ones getting scammed. Legitimate business owners are the ones who are the hardest hit by this. When these companies should be ranked number one or in another top spot, and are suddenly moved down the rankings, the calls that they receive drop drastically.

Then the scammers have the audacity to sell these hard working Americans their customers back to them at a markup. The whole arrangement has the distinct scent of a Mafia scam.

An easy way to look at it: THE MALL

This process might be easier to visualize if we compare it to something virtually everyone understands. To best describe all the different components of the problem, let's imagine a typical shopping mall. There are three different players in this scenario.

organization. Completely unrelated question: is there an emoji for "wink wink?"

The first is the consumers, being the shopping mall customers. The second is the businesses within the shopping mall; these represent the typical local businesses that you would find in your city.

The shopping mall itself represents a website like Google My Business, Bing Places, Yelp or Angie's list. Many people overlook the fact that the shopping mall is a business and has employees and management just like any other business. So to describe the problem, let's visualize how the various components at a shopping mall interrelate.

The shopping mall provides customers with easy access to many local businesses in one spot, similar to what the phone book did and what websites do now. Customers want the most relevant results, ultimately because they want to find what they are looking for as quickly and easily as possible.

In this shopping mall, however, there aren't just clothing and shoe stores, but organized hallways with different kinds of businesses; all separated by category. Think about how the phone book had different sections listed alphabetically. In this hypothetical mall, there is one hallway that has attorneys, carpet cleaners in another, and so on.

When you walk down one of the halls, the best local businesses in each category are sorted by various criteria, and moved toward the front, with the worst performing companies in the back. The criteria are unclear to the consumers, but you notice that the businesses with lots of reviews, flashy pictures, loud signs and websites tend to be closer to the front.

The reason that the shopping mall organizes these businesses this way is so that consumers are able to find the best local businesses in their city faster than just randomly picking a name out of a list. Most consumers would agree that this is a great way to set up results, as it rewards companies who do great work. Amazon does it with books, clothes and electronics, and allows customers to sort by average review, number of reviews and other criteria. Google and most other sites don't let you sort by those factors, but they do show them.

Have you ever needed a locksmith or a plumber? Usually when you need a locksmith, it's not some leisurely phone call for something that you need to cross off your to do list. ("Hi, I'm calling to schedule my semi-annual lock change. Sure, I'll hold.") A call to the locksmith generally means EMERGENCY and you need someone right away. I chose locksmith over plumber because the resulting hypothetical situation is far more disgusting in the plumbing example.[9]

So now imagine a consumer, parking and running into the shopping mall, trying to find the hallway of locksmiths, and now think about how she[10] is going to make her selection. Is this

---

[9]On account of the poop.

[10]I choose a woman for my hypothetical because hypothetical people in books used to always be male, which was sexist. Does this mean I have cured sexism? I

consumer going to do her due diligence and check the pricing of various locksmiths, asking to see business license information or references? In all likelihood, she is going to be running into the store right at the front. Because after all, she knows that the shopping mall knows what it is doing, puts the best and most reliable ones up front, and does so because it benefits both the mall and its customers.

Let's talk about the previous scenarios again, this time in the context of the shopping mall analogy.

Scenario 1

There are malls that organize businesses in every single city in the country. Realizing this fact, Joe Frauderson creates a "fake" business in the mall in Los Angeles so that he gets business in that city as well, without being licensed or properly established. The shopping malls do nothing to check the legal business status of their tenants; they only worry about whether the rent arrives on time. And it does... lots of it.

Scenario 2

Joe creates 30 fake businesses in 30 different malls. Instead of cleaning the pools himself, when a customer walks into his stores to get service, he calls one of the other stores in the mall and sells that store the customer's information. Joe could be the first pool cleaner in the hallway of pool cleaners, and thus would get most of the

let you decide.

traffic. Whenever they walk into one of Joe's fake shops, they are not going to get Joe the pool cleaner; the person who shows up to clean their pool could be any one of the actual pool cleaners in that mall. The only reason they are going to Joe is because Joe is better at figuring out the rules and criteria that the shopping mall uses to assign ranking to its local businesses. All Joe has to do is tell the pool cleaners that he has too much business, and since they are not getting as much business as usual, they are happy for the extra work, despite the cost.

Scenario 3

Joe defrauds a customer and customer complains. When she comes back to the mall with the police, the store is gone, and a different one is in its place. Where did Joe go? How are you going to find him, when that was the only place that he existed in the first place?

Here is where things get a little more interesting. The hypothetical shopping mall landlords know about this situation, and other than very basic and ineffectual measures that don't work, they do nothing about it. This isn't a new problem; the management and staff have been emailed, called, interviewed and hounded by people for years about these problems. And yet to this day, thousands of fake businesses continue to exist everywhere.

The malls in every city are owned by the same few management companies. Instead of fixing the problem, they rely too much on automation and other tools that are not really designed to combat the ingenuity and persistence of these criminals.

Of course, if Joe defrauded you, the person you'd be most upset with is Joe. But wouldn't at least some of your ire be directed at the owners of the mall? Wouldn't you want them to take steps to make sure that they aren't tacitly facilitating innumerable crimes like this? Especially if, you know, the landlord of that mall was about to be worth a TRILLION dollars?

That's all I'm saying.

Overall Thoughts

These shady characters do not create, innovate, or add value to anything. They are a plague and the problem is out of control. The organization[11] that I show you in Chapter 9 had 3000+ fake listings online on Google Maps alone at one time. Most of them were eventually taken down by automated spam detection processes, but many of them pop back up, and almost all of them still exist on other top directories.

This company is just in one industry, auto glass repair. Fake listings dominate nearly every service business category, putting real companies out of business because they simply cannot compete with the fake companies. Imagine losing your home, your job, and your livelihood because people with the power to stop the fraud deliberately ignore the problem and your cries for help?

---

[11]Hypothetical organization.

Go back to the story about the shopping mall. These scammers and criminals are taking business owners' rightful spots, procuring leads and selling them back at a markup. They might as well be coming into your home, stealing your television and then knocking on your door to sell it back to you. Are you just going to sit there and pay them because no one will do anything about it?

Imagine posting in help forums and getting no help from the staff and other websites other than "they will look into it." There are virtually no support chat lines for business owners who are having problems or consumers who were swindled.

As a business owner, you would think that you would have a way to report the spam that you find online. Google, for example, has historically touted its "report a problem" link to report spam. But the link only works on business listings that display their physical address. The fake listings typically have their addresses hidden because the scammers don't want people to be able to report them, and are hiding behind this glaringly obvious loophole has existed for more than two years.

Sometimes, stories make it into the news where shady locksmiths scam people or business owners are victimized by spam. In one case, there was a restaurant that had its business hours changed to show it being closed for the weekend. It cost them so much business that they had to close. Someone was able to edit this businesses listing without permission, and effectively ruined the owner's livelihood. Perhaps a jealous local business, angry customer or other malicious individual decided they should lose everything they worked so hard for. The restaurant was featured in the New York Times and yet nothing was done to fix it.

Commercial listings on the Internet are rife with not only inaccuracies, but intentionally misleading information designed to cheat you. Period. You are not getting fair representation or the chance to live the American dream in these conditions. If you own (or work for) a business that provides services that are listed earlier in this chapter, you should know that you are being held back by thieves, cheats, liars and worst of all, the companies that profit from delivering you this information in the first place.

Things should be different. They can be. Let me explain how.

Two

The Scammers

"I had been trained to rip people off and I was charging three times more than legitimate locksmiths were."

-Scammer who wished to remain unnamed

Scammers are the people who are collectively ruining thousands of small businesses across the United States and the world. They come from different backgrounds, business types, professions and are of all different types of race, creed or religion[12]. There is no one type of person that this problem can be pinned on, and that is one of the factors that makes the problem so hard to solve.

This chapter will explain who the scammers are, what businesses they operate in, and how they got into this type of "work". Some of them aim to defraud from the start; others are smart entrepreneurs who discovered ways to increase their market share and gradually became progressively more evil until it was too late to come back from it.[13] Money motivates all of us to some degree, but when

---

[12]Except the Amish.

money is one's sole priority, morality has no role in decision-making.

Two Types of Business Models for Scammers

The scammers in this book can be categorized a variety of ways. At its most simple level, there are two different business models in which they operate.

First Model: The Fakers

The first category is people who set up a business online and pretend to be a legal company. They answer the phone, respond to customers, provide the service the customer asked for, and collect money for their services. They're just not licensed, bonded, and insured. If they do a great job, then no harm, no foul (unless you're the government trying to collect taxes). And if they do a terrible job, or they steal everything out of your house instead of cutting your grass, you have zero practical recourse because you have no idea who they really are. All of the Internet presence that led you to them in the first place is fictitious.

Second Model: The Invisible Middlemen

The second type of scammer is also not a real business. But they're actually not even doing the service call. This makes it harder to catch them or even to identify them. They're generally running call centers and creating listings all over the country. When someone

---

[13]See Star Wars Episodes I-III. Better yet, don't.

calls the phone number on one of their bogus listings, the call is automatically (and undetectably) forwarded to a real business. When that company answers the call, the customer has no idea that they were automatically forwarded.

The phone system used to forward the calls also tracks the phone calls and times of each call. The scammer in control of the phone number knows who called, when they called, and usually records all of the calls. On a side note, just the act of recording the call for tracking purposes is *extremely* illegal; like gay marriage in Mississippi.[14] The customer is typically not warned that the call is being recorded, and the receptionist is usually not aware either. It's like the old time party lines of the 1980's, except slightly even more sad.

When the legitimate company shows up, they perform the work, and bill the customer. You called *First Search Results Plumbing* and *Somebody Else Plumbing* showed up. This is not inherently problematic, but many problems can and do stem from it.

The scammer then analyzes the data and figures out how many calls were transferred to the company receiving the calls. Let's say that each call costs $10 (this is one of the lower priced calls, some calls are worth $50-$100 each, depending on the industry), and the company transferred 500 calls. They send a bill for $5000…just for providing the "service" of intercepting your business between the search engine and the legitimate businesses that were hoping you

---

[14]Through June 2015.

would call them directly and unwiretappedly. But does this legitimate business report the middleman to the appropriate authorities? As Abraham Lincoln said at Ford's Theater, "hellz, no". They are all too happy to pay, because they made far more than $5000 off of the leads that were provided.

Most of the time, the company that is receiving the leads has no idea that they are receiving bogus calls. Generally the scammers call them offering them overflow calls[15] from their own business, or that the calls came from websites or somewhere else. The company paying for these leads has no idea how the customers were "created", but they are more than happy for the extra business. And besides; even if they are skeptical about the source, they know that if they don't buy the leads, one of their competitors will. Like elsewhere in this cancerous ecosystem, the people making money don't stop to analyze where it comes from; they just sign the back of the checks and go back to trying to feed their families.

Not to belabor the point, but let me belabor the point. If the scammers were prevented from placing their listings into the search engines, then legitimate businesses would be at the top of the search results. The listings would be organized based on legitimate, objective criteria such as popularity and real reviews (we'll cover the review process later). The just would be rewarded, and the

---

[15]In the plumbing industry, this idiom carries a hilarious double meaning. Yes, another poop joke.

legitimate businesses would make more profit while the consumers paid lower prices. Kind of a nice idea, right?

How big are these spammer organizations?

As we discuss the size and scope of these organizations, perhaps the best analogy is to think of them like movie popcorn. They can be broken down into three different sizes; let's arbitrarily call them "small", "medium", and (you guessed it) "large". But the "small" is actually quite large, the "large" is obscene, and you're paying too much no matter what size you deal with.

There is a difference between the ethics and priorities of the small, medium and large scammers. Many of the people in the medium and large-scale groups started out small, but as their desire to expand and generate more income grew, they became more and more willing to make "compromises".[16] But by the time a scammer has become large, there is no amount of pretending that can hide the fact that they are deliberately and intentionally defrauding customers, stealing business from legitimate companies and ultimately running an entire business model based around cheating the general public out of its hard-earned money.[17]

Small Scale Scammers

There are many brilliant and savvy small business owners throughout this country who have adapted intelligently to the Internet age. Social media, digital advertising and other avenues are

[16]Like Marlon Brando.
[17]Like in "The Freshman".

designed for the sole purpose of guiding customers to the business they are looking for.

Every major directory or mapping service online is constantly innovating and striving to provide the most relevant results in the hopes that their customers are able to find the content they want, so they visit that same search engine again the next time they look for something. Google Maps has the highest market share of the maps services. Apple Maps, Bing Maps and Yelp are not far behind, and collectively have over 99% of all local searches come through them.

Here's a real world example of what a customer ("or end-user") would experience when conducting a local search. This sounds a lot more complicated than it really is, because in reality no one thinks:

> "Hey, I am going to conduct a local search. I'd better get out my computing device, get on the Internet, and enter a query so that I am able to find the information that I am looking for. I have all the time in the world, so I will select a business the way a fame whore on ABC chooses a fiancé; with painstaking care."

In reality, a single mother has a pipe burst at her bakery. She is stressed enough as it is (don't get her started on her baby daddy). There is water all over the floor, the equipment is beginning to get damaged and she needs a plumber. She pulls out her phone, types *plumber in dallas*[18] and calls the first plumber on the list. Twenty

---

[18]Her bakery is in Dallas in this example. (Not all the footnotes have obscure jokes.)

minutes goes by, someone shows up, fixes the leak, collects payment and leaves. This happens every day in businesses all across the country.

The entire marketing industry revolves around one simple concept that is fundamental to understanding how someone crosses the line to committing fraud. If your business can generate more website hits, that means more phone calls from customers, and that means your company will make more money. It absolutely is that simple.

Getting people to go to your website is the hardest part. Millions of companies offer a variety of solutions to accomplish this goal. Yet to date, no one can give you any assurances as to what your return on investment will be if you spend x dollars on advertising through them. Television commercials, radio advertising, flyers, emails, promotions, newspaper ads, Google Adwords and Adsense; they're all a roll of the dice. And like when you roll the dice in Vegas, you might win. The people who own the dice *always* win.

But what if you could market your company for *free*? Instead of risking your hard earned money in the hopes that you can make more through marketing, now your advertising becomes a no risk proposition. It either attracts new customers or it doesn't. Enter the Internet.[19]

If you look at the top ten listings on Google Maps,[20] the ones in the top three will get an overwhelming majority of the phone calls and

---

[19]But not in a *Tron* way.

website hits. Customers are not going to call all ten on the first page; they might call two and then pick the cheapest of them. They will call the ones at the top, *because* they are at the top.

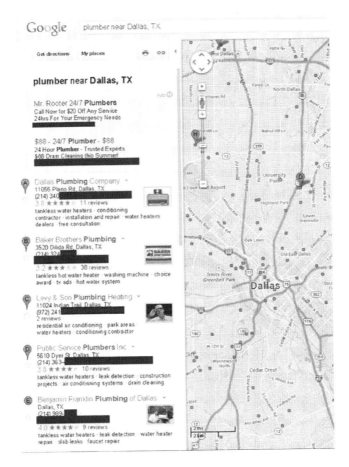

Figure 2.1[21]

[20]For example. Allegedly.

[21]This screen shot is used for illustrative purposes only. We do not claim to know which business on this shot are real and which ones are not. So if your business is listed here, don't sue us. Just thank us for the free advertising and go about your day.

Imagine you are a business owner and you are in the 7th spot. You know that you want to be in the top three. So you fabricate some reviews from some fake accounts, add some keywords to your listing, polish up your website and read guides online for how to increase your "ranking" on Google Maps. A couple of hours later, you are in the top three, and you immediately notice a huge surge in calls that doesn't go away. A once struggling carpet cleaning company is now flush with cash because of a few simple keystrokes and good advice.

This is the point where many people realize that they could get a second location for their business in this virtual world without having to open a new physical location. They have an office, but no one shows up. Because let's face it, when was the last time you went to your landscaper's office? What about your pool cleaner? You call them and they come to you, so what would it take to open a second location, when all of your business is coming from Google, Bing, Apple and Yelp?

You follow the same procedure to get your business listed on Google Maps; this time using a friend's address across town. It was set up the same way as the first location, but with a second phone number that is forwarding calls to your cell phone. Nearly overnight, your phone call volume increases. Your business grows, you buy more trucks, hire more employees, and cash more checks. But half of your business was created by a lie. Half of it was stolen. Half of it was fraud.

Was it really fraud, you might ask? Well, did you file for a second business license? Is it really a place that you are doing business? Are all the reviews real? When you cut corners, it is not legal or ethical.

Thousands of small business owners have figured this out. It is exceedingly simple to do. Most people have a home address, or a family member who lives in a different part of town, and being able to cover more area or territory nearly instantly generates more income.

Now the real question is, once you know that two locations are better than one, will you be stopping at just two? Most don't. In that way, business locations are like potato chips.

To give you an idea of what kind of money we're talking about by adding just one duplicate business, a service-based company can easily double its annual revenue. Imagine that every single phone call that it receives is worth $10. Now let's take the average amount of calls that this business gets per week; let's say 300. That is $3000 per week in income that is coming in to the business already. That comes out to $156,000 a year. Are you telling me that you would turn down $300,000 a year when all it takes is two hours of work to set up a fake business phone number and simple website?

Medium Sized Scammers

Medium sized scammers are often small businesses owners in service industries who realized a while ago that one location was not enough for their income requirements. So they added more locations that they are able to effectively service. Think of a pool cleaning company that services a county and has one location in each city within that county. That could be 30 or even 40 locations. It is important to note that this is all the same business, and possibly even the same business name, so as to maintain brand recognition. It would be the hope that they could market their company, so when customers look for "Abe's Log Cabin Repair" they are quickly able to find one in their city.

Cities have taxes as well as states and the federal government. But if you open a phantom location in Town Y, and only pay taxes in Town X, you are enriching X at the cost of Y. It's just another hidden cost of the lies.

This is also the point at which enterprising individuals realize that there is a huge market for phone calls and generating calls for businesses that they can simply sell instead of service. As we just talked about, businesses want to receive more phone calls because the phone calls generate income. Therefore a phone call from a customer is inherently worth money. What this monetary value is depends entirely on the type of business.

A phone call from a customer wanting a pool cleaner is more valuable than a phone call for a minor home repair. Why? A pool cleaning call is going to be an ongoing client. One pool is worth around $1,000 to a pool cleaner. They can sell that client to another pool cleaner for that price all day long. The calls that are often worth the most are customers looking for a locksmith. These are customers that need help NOW, and are desperate to get into whatever it is that they locked themselves out of. Perhaps it's a hot car with their baby inside, or their home at the end of a hard day's work. The calls are also extremely valuable because locksmiths charge a high amount for their services, but have very small costs (also known as "profit margin" for you nerd types). A single phone call for a locksmith is worth over $50 per call. For a locksmith with no employees, the leads are generally literally their most valuable asset…and thus can be their largest expense.

Let's say that you don't own a locksmith company, but you know people who do. Instead of being good at the service, you realize that you are good with the Internet and decide you are going to generate leads. Generating the leads isn't difficult when you can just create a business out of thin air. It starts with 5 or 10 locations throughout your metro area, and pretty soon you are generating hundreds of calls that you forward directly to your locksmith friend. He is ecstatic at the increase in business and is writing you checks every single week for the calls you refer to him.

You have built a business entirely based on fraud and did not even need to get out of your chair. Thousands of dollars are coming in every week, and you begin hiring staff to help you create more and more. Reviews need to be added, rankings of your listings tracked, and it's not hard to expand when you don't have to open any brick and mortar stores.

To summarize, the people in this category are in two distinct groups with similar profiles. There is the savvy business owner who has expanded his business virtually, but in reality has only one or two locations. Then there is the "lead generation" company that doesn't actually exist in reality at all. This is by far the more dangerous of the two, because it is this type of scammer that is not bound by conscience at all. This is the type of scammer that turns into the large scammer quickly, as things grow and they get more ambitious.

Large Scale Scammers

The large scammers are much fewer than those in the first two categories. Almost every large scammer organization is well organized, run in most respects like a legitimate business, and generally started as a medium sized scammer.

Large spammers can focus on one industry, but have a huge reach. Imagine thousands of businesses all across the country, with different business names, unique websites, and even call centers supporting the inbound phone calls. A customer calls, asks for a quote or for someone to come to their location, and would never know that this is a fake company. How could they? Someone answers the phone "Auto Glass, how may I help you?" which is exactly who they intended to call. In many cases, a customer can look at the top ten results and six of them are the same company masquerading as a real company. All different business names, numbers, reviews, and websites, and the customers are completely in the dark.

Another business model that the large scammers use is diversification. They generate phone calls with fake listings in multiple industries to avoid having their entire business shut down because of a mistake or security crackdown. Since there are so many different kinds of businesses to choose from, the market is virtually unlimited. The types of businesses are always service-based businesses that go to where the customer is. There are easily 50+ industries where scammers flourish because of this very simple concept. We see the trucks on the roads, and we assume they have a building or an office where they keep their plumbs and landscapes. Are they legitimate? Did you check their business license? What about their bonding and insurance status?

Company example number 1: a large-scale garage door sales and repair company in Southern California. Let's call them "Bryan Seely Is Handsome Garage Door Repair". This company owns its own manufacturing and distribution warehouse that supplies new equipment and replacement parts for technicians in Southern California. The parts are cheap, made in China and are not up to code. The problem with this is when you look and see a garage door repair listing near your house, the convenience factor outweighs any possible indication that this could be a fake business. Americans believe that most companies will do a job right, and that if there's a problem, that they will have recourse with the government. After all, if you see a commercial on television, or hear one on the radio, the government ensures that the information is accurate. So why not online?

In order to create these fake listings at a large scale, the company would typically hire someone who knows how to manipulate the search engines and pay them on a per listing basis. They would order 1000 locations and provide the desired business name, city, phone number and sometimes even the desired address. The scammer would then build all of these listings for a fee; typically around $10-$20 for each location, or $10,000-$20,000 for the thousand locations you want. Not too bad for a couple days work.

This company now has 1000 "locations". Now imagine that each of these locations gets just one call per day. ONE. A phone call to a garage door repair company is worth around $20 for a repair; up to $50 or more for a new installation. Since this company is generating its own leads and servicing them as well, they are making all of the profits and do not have to pay for the costs per call.

One thing to think about is the scale in which you can build these businesses. There are roughly 300 cities in the United States that have a population over 100,000 people. There are approximately 1000 cities in the United States that have 30,000 people or more. Generally with a city size of around 100,000 people you can have two or three business listings without having too much overlap. So consider the 1000 listings spread throughout the entire United States. All of the phone calls go to a call center and when a job is requested the call center dispatches a technician from that location to the customer.

From the customer standpoint, there's nothing different on their end. They call the company, wait for a little while, and then someone shows up to perform the work that they requested. To them, the job is done. Did it really matter if that person had a business license? Would it matter if that person were a sex offender? Did you let him in your house?

If a company like this has 1000 locations, they will probably average around 1000 calls a week. As they get better at what they do, perhaps they will increase their volume to 2000 calls per week. That is over 100,000 phone calls per year. If they were buying those leads at $10 each, they would've paid $1,000,000 for them. And they got them for the initial fee of $10,000.

Actual Scammers

As explained above, the people who are drawn to this industry do not fit one specific race, creed or geographic location. The only thing that they share is a way to game the system and indifference to the harm that it causes others. Some of the people in the smaller category may not even realize that there are actual victims in this crime.

The majority of the spammers are individuals who live in anywhere from the United States, the Philippines, Israel, Russia, Europe and across the globe.

There are literally thousands of people making a living this way. I don't say "make a living" to make them sound endearing or noble. Rather, they want to make money in any way possible. This is a way that they can accomplish that goal from the comfort of their home without ever having to leave their chairs.

Where do they learn about this stuff?

There are a variety of forums that talk about different blackhat techniques that are available online. People sell the information. Some make videos. Others make PDF's and presentations. They do webinars and sell the information for anywhere between $100 to thousands of dollars. So generally, when someone wants to learn this type of technique, it isn't that hard to find. There are even videos on YouTube. Where there's ill will, there's a way.

Just as there is a problem with getting the search engines to remove spam in their maps product, there is the same problem with Youtube and other places. We will dissect the problem from a legal perspective later, but in short: under the existing laws, these websites are generally on safer legal ground doing *nothing* than doing something. If you have a pool in your back yard, you are allowed to put up as sign that says "no trespassers". If someone breaks into your house and drowns, chances are very small that you'll be sued. But if you hire a lifeguard for your pool, he'd better know CPR.

And it's not like you can just call the police and say, "Hey, someone has this video on YouTube that's potentially doing something wrong." Well, you can. Just don't expect anything to happen.

So someone stumbles upon a YouTube video or forum post that advertises a way to hack the search directories that costs $100. Suddenly they have access to a private video and learn how to create a fake listing. They then get access to a private video and learn how to create a fake listing. As discussed in a later chapter, there are many ways to accomplish this and scammers will usually pick the one that works for them. There's never a shortage of people looking for a search engine hacker.

Profile of an Actual Scammer #1

Due to fear of retaliation, this individual requested that we not include any identifying information about him or the area he works.

> "I came to the United States from [redacted] in middle east with a childhood friend, around the same time, 20 years ago. We both moved to the redacted US city area, but both choose very different paths. He is one of the biggest spammers in the country, but has long since left the United States. Before there was Google maps, he was a spammer on the 411 directory listings and Yellow Pages. He would register phone numbers and fake businesses all over the country and anytime people would call 411, they would usually get one of his businesses. He was making around 20 million dollars a year for over a decade and now travels the world with his family.

We lived in the same part of redacted country in middle east as a kid, but chose much different path. I always thought he would get caught, but he never did. He didn't just manipulate the directories in the US, but in Europe and Canada as well. There is just so much money in the scamming business."

Profile of an Actual Scammer #2

Due to fear of retaliation, this scammer requested that we not include any identifying information about him or the area he works.

"It all started when I worked for a locksmith scammer, one of those who is responsible for locksmith spam on Google Maps. I didn't know that they were scammers at the time, I thought that it was only high pressure sales tactics as seen on the floor of department stores and car lots that I was engaging in.

I soon discovered that I had been trained to rip people off and that I was charging three times more than legitimate locksmiths were. I was ashamed and as soon as I was able to find another source of income I left the business of locksmith scamming, and resolved to make sure I did everything I could to stop them from ripping off more people to atone for the part I played in the scheme. (In six months I made them $20,000.)

That was when I started my own locksmith business with fixed rates to undercut the scammers and beat them at their own game. I got my business name out on all of the same places they put theirs, including Google Adwords and Google Maps.

My business was taken to be locksmith spam by somebody and was removed, and that is what launched me into Google Mapmaker and fighting spam. I failed to reinstate my own listing, and figured if mine got deleted then I could get the fake locksmiths deleted just as easily.

I spent perhaps three or four hours every week, at times marking for deletion all of the locksmith spam in the state of [redacted] over a weekend using tricks taught to me by Dan Austin. I got a ton of spam removed, tens of thousands of listings through reporting it on a spreadsheet used by the Google Maps spam team.

Then Google made it harder to report. They ignored the spreadsheet. I started riding around to spam listings on my motorcycle and using photo documentation as well as informing the owners of the addresses in question that locksmith scam artists were fraudulently using their addresses, and gave them a Google case number so that they could express directly to Google what they thought of it.

One particular locksmith listing I reported to Google really bothered me because these guys were posing as me and other locksmiths in the area and ripping people off. I went to their listed address, took pictures of the locked door that violated the Google Places for Business TOS, took pictures of the call box that showed no locksmith anywhere next to the phone numbers, and reported it on the Google places for business forums. Google never deleted it.

I kept insisting and posting back on that thread that there was no business open during business hours and that it should be deleted, but there it is today. I posted pictures of the actual apartment door that is listed as the business headquarters on the state of [redacted] business license website, but to no avail.

Today I have given up on fighting spam on Google Maps. I instead concentrate on informing people that have been ripped off on Google's complicity in the matter, and helping people to report the individuals who personally ripped them off by helping them file complaints with the state authorities. I also use a phone number anonymizer to call the scammers and get them to drive to far away places.

When they call me to say they are there to help me, I tell them to get real jobs and stop ripping people off, I report their phone numbers, and I erase the phone number. I do this to dishearten the scammers, waste their time so hopefully they won't rip some other person off, and also in case they are like me and don't know they are ripping people off.

I hope that you will use the information I have given you anonymously, as the scammers would no doubt dislike me immensely if they knew from where the light is shining on them in [redacted]. If you want information about how the locksmith scammers operate I am happy to give you the insiders' perspective and help you illuminate others on this topic in any way I can."

Profile of an Actual Scammer #3

To give you an idea what kind of lengths these people will use to scam the public, some of them will even use semi-legal tactics to manipulate and scam the public. Here is a list of names that one single scammer registered within one state.[22]

- # 24 HOUR LOCKSMITH Active N/A 01/11/2008
- # LOCKSMITH 24 HOUR Active N/A 01/11/2008 0 0 0
- A LOCKSMITH SERVICE Active N/A 01/11/2008
- 007 LOCKS & LOCKSMITH SERVICE Active N/A 08/08/2008
- 1 2 3 24/7 LOCKSMITH SERVICE Active N/A 08/08/2008
- 1 24 HOUR LOCKSMITH Active N/A 01/11/2008
- 1 EMERGENCY LOCKSMITH Active N/A 01/11/2008
- 1 VANCOUVER EMERGENCY LOCKSMITH Active N/A 01/11/2008
- 1ST 24 HOUR TOWING Active N/A 08/09/2011
- 24 / 7 LOCKSMITH Active N/A 08/08/2008
- A 24 / 7 LOCKSMITH Active N/A 08/08/2008
- A EMERGENCY LOCKSMITH Active N/A 08/08/2008
- A FAST LOCKSMITH SERVICE Active N/A 08/08/2008
- A FULL SERVICE LOCKSMITH Active N/A 08/08/2008
- A LOCKS & LOCKSMITH 24/7 Active N/A 08/08/2008

---

[22]That doesn't mean that there aren't legitimate locksmiths operating under one or more of these names.

- A LOCKSMITH SERVICE Active N/A 01/11/2008
- A RE-KEY LOCKSMITH 24 / 7 Active N/A 08/08/2008
- A RESIDENTIAL & COMMERCIAL
  LOCKSMITH Active N/A 08/08/2008
- EMERGENCY LOCKSMITH Active N/A 01/11/2008
- LOCKS & LOCKSMITH SERVICE Active N/A 01/11/2008
- LOCKSMITH SERVICE Active N/A 01/11/2008

Adwords; the Problem Worsens

One recent development in the protocols of many search engines is the elevation of listings that expressly pay money to be at the top of search results. As you might expect, this makes it even more straightforward for scammers to manipulate the listings...and even easier for the search engine companies to directly profit from misinformation.

Look at this example:

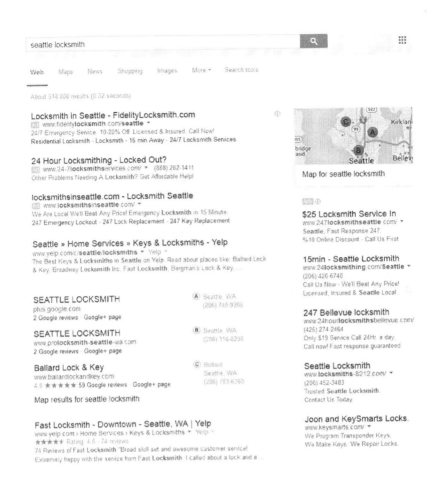

Figure 2.2

This page of search results includes listings that are derived from the basic algorithms, and some that are paid for. The paid listings are now displayed with the yellow identifier "Ad". This is very useful information to display.

From the perspective of the search engines, it gives them some degree of disclosure that they have been paid to have that listing included. But throughout the history of media, there have been advertisements. And the honesty of what is included in those advertisements has been subject to oversight and not just by the government, but also by media outlets that publish them. (For a good laugh, research cigarette ads from the 1950's and learn all about their "health benefits".)

But that is not the current state of the law on the Internet. Ironically, the "Ad" designation online tends to make a listing *more* likely to be fake. Somebody paid to have it there, nobody is responsible for the truth of the claims, and lies make more money than truth. So you follow an ad in a service industry at your peril.

As the years have gone by, the scammers' playground that is online search engines has changed by adding products or ineffectual security protocols, but the most recent development that is hugely devastating is how scammers are finding their victims.

To give you a brief summary, scammers are using advertising to execute what is called "bait and switch" tactics to scam customers. What this means is, they are baiting customers with extremely low prices, and when they show up, "switching" the cost considerably and saying that they had some sort of special circumstance or issue that is more expensive. The problem is that the prices advertised are so incredibly low and people call them over and over and over again. You know from a lifetime of experience roughly what a case of Coke costs. If you saw one advertised for $.05, you'd likely be skeptical. But because most people have little experience with hiring a locksmith, they have no sense of just what an absurd price $19 is for a locksmithing service, and just how unlikely it is that such an offer is legitimate.

One locksmith that we spoke with said that he has seen scamming locksmiths paying hundreds of thousands of dollars a month into the Google Adwords program that controls these advertisements.

This is a very big problem, and we will be addressing it in depth in a later chapter, as several search engines were sued in federal court for millions by a legitimate locksmith in Virginia. (Spoiler alert: Goliath won.)

It becomes difficult to try and identify the very small scammers because typically they are running a legitimate operation and then add one or two false locations to increase sales. Most people don't see the ethical dilemma immediately. Some take even longer to realize that they are not only lying to their own customers but stealing from other businesses.

Many people rationalize this behavior by saying "everyone else is doing it". In reality, this is not true at all. There are millions of businesses throughout this country that are competing fairly and not taking shortcuts in order to make a few (or even a few million) more bucks.

However, let's be clear: businesses fail because they could not keep up with the scammers. The millions they take out of the legitimate business ecosystem have a devastating cost. We have the power to stop it. We need to exercise that power.

Three

The Victims

Before you can decide how much to care about the issue of Internet fraud, and how much you're willing to do to bring about change, you have to understand precisely who the victims are, and how much they are harmed. The answers to these questions are "every taxpayer in the United States, for a start" and "billions of dollars a year". Bold claims require bold proof. Here is the proof.

There are several categories of victims; this chapter will discuss each in turn.

Scammed Consumers

As discussed in Chapter 1, many of the scams that have arisen from the Internet seem ridiculously easy to spot. Remember the good laugh we had talking about the Nigerian prince scam? Because generally the scams that get the most attention are the brazen ones that only prey on the most gullible, it would be easy to conclude that the consumers victimized deserve what happens to them on some level, and therefore that they are not fully worthy of our sympathy.

This conclusion, while easy, is totally wrong. Although there are sensational crimes that garner headlines and even chuckles, the vast majority of consumers victimized by Internet fraud are people with little or no basis to suspect that they are at risk of being cheated. This can be because the scammers are just that good or because the consumers think they have no reason to question the authenticity of a business listed through a reputable website.

We've already discussed the non-hypothetical hypothetical of the person who needs a locksmith. She gets reeled in by an offer to change a lock for $15; then, when the technician arrives, the price is $150. What do they do? More often than not, they pay it. Perhaps they think that they can get their money back. Sure, this locksmith is a scammer. But when his boss, or the government, hears about this, I'll get my money back.

If only it were that simple.

If you're scammed by a fake business, the fake business isn't scared of what you can do to it. Go ahead, the scammer says: call the Better Business Bureau, email the local news, file an insurance claim, picket, post signs, or even dial 911. He's already thought all of your options, and he's happy to let you choose one.

When the business is fake, it is typically not registered anywhere but on the website search engine where you found it. All they have to do is change their number and move on. With police and most of the general public completely in the dark about this issue, their boldness is justified. Stories have made it into the media all over the country about locksmith and other types of scammers, but ultimately nothing happens. There have been major media outlets covering these types of stories after frustrated consumers have reported it, but change remains elusive. Here are some examples.

MyFoxMemphis-Jan 14th, 2015: Hollis knew something was up when the supposed locksmith who showed up to change the locks on the business and then tried to charge her way more than   expected.

"It was three times the amount, it got up to about $292," Hollis said. The original price she was quoted from Town & Country Locksmiths was around $105. Then she started noticing other red flags. The guy in her store did not work for the company she originally called (Town & Country Locksmiths).[xiii]

Palm Beach Daily News - August 25th, 2013: An impostor who police say has been scamming his customers, including many from Palm Beach, with an organized fraudulent locksmith operation turned himself in Wednesday.

David Merkatz, 55, was the scam's "mastermind," police said. Merkatz would advertise in telephone directories and on the Internet using false information, identifying himself as a locksmith from legitimate companies, according to police.[xiv]

The Sacramento Bee - October 26th, 2014: More than two hours later, in the dark, the locksmith showed up, she said, "in an unmarked truck and wasn't wearing a uniform. There was nothing that showed he was a locksmith."

He quickly popped open her locked security screen door, then drilled out her front door lock and replaced it with a simple "bedroom doorknob," according to Boyle.

All the work was completed in about 15 minutes, said Boyle, a state employee. But instead of the $19 service call and an "online discount" quoted in the ad, the final bill was $300. And despite what was said in the ad, the locksmith said he couldn't accept a credit card, only cash.[xv]

There are hundreds of these stories all over the Internet. Most of the time, these people don't have any clue that they're being scammed or that this is a fake business. Because 95% of the time these people call a "local business". They saw a map establishing their "location" was nearby and everything. The person shows up and says that they're there for whatever reason that they called for. And everyone assumes everything's fine. It doesn't even occur to them that there's a chance they're being scammed.

Most people wouldn't dream of looking up a business license for something as simple as a one-time service based transaction. Most people will just assume that it's verified as an authentic business; especially when companies have a little check mark that says something like "verified local business". Don't assume that the commercial information you see online is something you can trust like the ads on television. It absolutely is not.

Why would someone pay $200 when they were expecting to be charged $20?[23]

They might be afraid of their physical safety, or simply despise confrontation. Not everyone wants to challenge everything that they go through in a day. I mean, the person performed the service. Now they're jacking the price. It's not fair to pay *nothing*. He could be threatening to call the police for non-payment or perhaps threatening legal action. Where's the manual on what to do when a business does that? It's not something people deal with on a daily basis, or something that comes up in their regular life.

Most people are not lawyers or law enforcement, and when it is the word of one person versus the word of another, it's common to believe that there is no way to prove that a given thing happened. Especially when the person you have to accuse of being a fraud is someone entrusted with public safety. Locksmiths hold a position of power. You can give birth to a dispute that could last months or even years…or you can pay a couple hundred bucks and never have

---

[23]Later in this book you can read an anecdote someone told me about a Google employee who called a locksmith she found via a Google advertisement like the ones above, and who was scammed in Google's own parking lot. I don't know if it happened, but I sure believe it.

to think about it again. Every day, people are put in this situation. Every day, many of them just pay.

We have a moral obligation to fight back against the strong who prey upon the weak.

Legitimate Businesses

One layer below the individual consumers scammed, there are the legitimate businesses that suffer at the hands of these fake businesses. The concept is simple: every call that a fake business gets is a call that a legitimate business doesn't get. Or, as discussed in Chapter 1, sometimes it's both; the fake business fields the call and seamlessly forwards it to the legitimate business. And in exchange, the fake business takes a cut of the sale, or as they say in New Jersey, "wets its beak a little".

So how hard is it for a legitimate business in a service industry rife with scammers to get on the first page of a major search engine? Really quite difficult, actually.

Here is a screenshot from January of 2015.

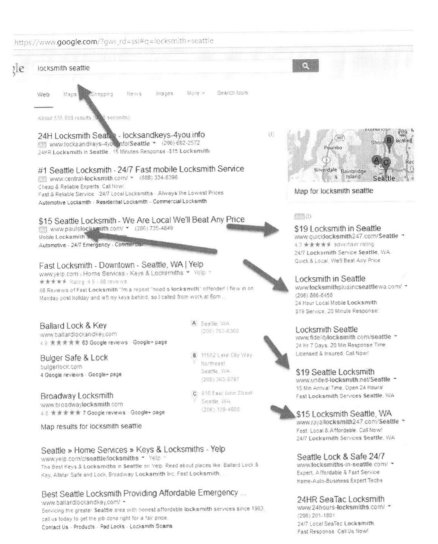

Figure 2.3

The businesses with the arrows pointing at them are advertising that they offer a $15 or $19 lockout special. This is almost certainly fraudulent advertising. There is no locksmith in this country that will come and unlock your car or your home for that price; unless they are trying to lose money as part of some elaborate wager.

Not to blame the victims, but just stop and think for a second: what possible motive could a locksmith have to change your lock for $15? That is not enough to cover the cost of gas and the pay for the technician doing the job. It's not like an industry with regular repeat business. One could imagine, for example, a pool cleaner giving you a break on your first cleaning in the hopes that you get hooked on their amazing scrubbing prowess and feed them for the long term. But how often do you need a locksmith? Exactly as often as you make a catastrophic mistake with your keys.

The businesses that you see pointed out on that screen shot above are, in all probability, scammers. This is a problem in every single major city in the country. Some of these locksmith organizations are small, 1-5 person operations with someone spending the money on these ads knowing the consumers will click. They will set up ads in the cities that they serve, and if they have to change their business name, they will do so if they get too many complaints. Typically they will have numerous DBA (doing business as) names, and run multiple websites and business listings so as to look like multiple companies.

So where does that leave legitimate locksmiths who can't afford all the web optimization techniques because they have other annoying expenses like paying for business licenses and employment taxes? Off the first page of search results and out of luck.

In Chapter 8, we will explore one such locksmith who fought back hard against the big boys, and tried to pick the metaphorical lock to the Fort Knox of their billions in revenue. Spoiler alert: Fort Knox has a security system. And pit bulls.

These victims are not just the small business owners, but also their employees and their families. A company's ability to pay wages is directly tied to its profit margins. Some companies make billions; most are just trying to make enough to pay a living wage and reward the owners for the risk they took to open the business in the first place. These businesses have survived recessions and other hard times, but this threat is one that many small businesses cannot withstand. I have spoken with many of these companies and in so many cases, they did not even realize what went wrong. Nowhere to place the blame, no way to fight back; all they knew was that their customer base got smaller and smaller, and the money that they were once making evaporated.

The businesses that are hardest hit are the ones that rely on phone calls from customers. These businesses rely on customers finding them through online search directories.

When a business like this does not get as many phone calls, it means that it does not have as many customers. That means less revenue. Less revenue means they will have to cut back on employees, equipment, and their piece of the American dream is at risk. Many times, they lost their homes and their entire livelihood because of these scammers.

But how?

In the simplest of terms, the scammers took all the top ranked spots on the search results pushed the rightful businesses out of the rankings. Businesses that are in the top 3 spots on a search page get around 90% of the calls. When scammers occupy those spots, the businesses that were formerly the biggest and most popular in the city suffer.

The Taxpayers and Tax Collectors

If one believes what one learned in school, Benjamin Franklin said that the only two certainties in life are death and taxes. Well, if Poor Richard's Almanac had been a blog, Ben might have cut the list in half.

This is because fake businesses pay no taxes. Without a business license, there is no mechanism through which they can pay local taxes. When the locksmith takes that cash from you, they aren't racing back to headquarters to hand-write out a receipt to send to the IRS.

Just imagine what the government could do with billions more in annual tax revenue. It could build, like, three more stealth bombers. (Hopefully you have a more vivid imagination than I do.)

No matter how wisely they spend it, all levels of our government have the right to this money. You pay taxes, so shouldn't your neighbor? A penny saved is a penny earned. Together, we can track down a lot of lost pennies.

Four

The Moderators

This chapter is about the people who are in charge of the websites discussed in this book. There are so many different websites that have a substantial reach, many of which you have used before or at least know about from advertisements or friends. Here are a few of the most well-known and largest websites:

- Google
- Bing
- Yahoo!
- Yelp
- WhitePages
- Angie's List

Keep in mind that the biggest and most popular sites are not the only ones that have a problem with fake data. Some of the websites and directories are doing a better job than others at providing "clean data" to their customers. Just as the companies who are willingly complicit in Internet fraud deserve public scrutiny, the companies that strive to eradicate false listings deserve praise.

One of the many benefits of being able to identify fraud is to be able to identify its absence. I have even included a rating system, so that you can make a more informed decision about what sites to visit online. Rather than speak unkindly about any particular company at this point (you're welcome, team of lawyers!), I will let the data speak for itself. (You can't sue data, can you?)

Data Sources

One of the challenges that these websites face is getting accurate data into their maps products. As you can probably imagine, there are a lot of businesses in the United States. Furthermore, though it is a little known fact in these parts, there are other countries in the world besides the United States.[24] Many of these countries (approximately 100%) also have businesses, and a desire to freely disseminate accurate business information. According to the U.S. Census Bureau, there were around 28 million businesses in the United States, with 27.9 million being defined as "small businesses".

That's an awful lot of businesses to keep track of; and the less web-savvy a business is, the harder it is for Internet resources to accurately catalog them. (Thought experiment: imagine a business with no website that does not voluntarily opt into White Pages or

---

[24]At least ten.

any similar list. How would the Internet know it exists? Only from sources that cull records that a business is required to maintain, such as a business license, or from what other people say about that business online.)

What search engine companies have learned is that they have to find data to provide content; the more data, the better. So they rely on a variety of means to accomplish their goals, but there are only two main sources: "End user" submitted data and "shared data" from other companies.

What is "end user data", you ask? I'm glad you asked. Who are end users? Simple: you, me, and everyone else. Think "Yelp". You experience a business, and you go online to talk about it. You're hoping that the world is listening to your rave review of your local diner, or your spite-filled rant about the dry cleaner that didn't get the stain out of your pants. Good news! Someone is listening…and exploiting you for profit.

By contrast, data shared from other companies does not come from end users like you and me. There are plenty of things wrong with end user data. It's subjective and it's easily faked, but it has at least one thing going for it: except for some bizarre hypotheticals we could invent, it's pretty much always voluntary. But there are other ways that people can learn things besides viewing something a person jotted down on a keyboard to proliferate information voluntarily. Indeed, if you think about it, in the modern age, we are each, in essence, a never-ending stream of data, leaking uncontrollably down the leg of the Internet (which explains the smell). That data has value from being known to others…so others collect it. (Think of a large metaphorical plastic cup with a sealable lid.)

Let's pretend that we want to start a company that rivals Google Maps. (We don't, but plenty of people do.) That's going to be one empty website without all the business information. So now we have to figure out how to get that data. According to David Mihm at Moz.com:

"In the United States, there are four primary sources of data for all the major search engines: Infogroup, Acxiom, Localeze, and Factual.

Other companies like Yellowpages, Citysearch, and Superpages can also play a role in this cycle, sending "fresh" feeds to the search engines every couple of months.[xvi]"

Google Maps (they have changed their name quite a few times, so in this next graphic you will see it called "Google + Local") gets its information from a few places.

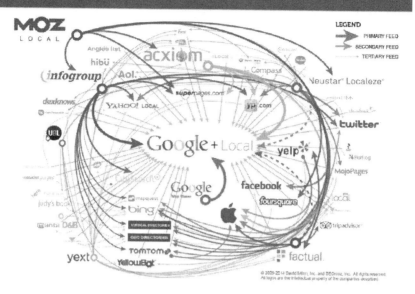

Figure 4.1 For illustrative purposes only. Copyright David Mihm, Inc and SEOmoz, Inc. All rights reserved. All logos are the intellectual property of the companies shown. [xvii]

Reviewing the above, you can learn quite a bit about who gets information from where. Like with any ecosystem, there is a lot of interconnectivity.

As all of these websites and partners have figured out that sharing data is really important to their business model. They all want to provide current data to their customers so that when you go to Google Maps, you can see data from all of these providers in one spot. The end user has no idea who originated the data, as it is presented to you as a part of the website you are looking at currently. If no one shared data, it would be nearly impossible for end users to figure out what website to use to find accurate local business information. For example, a search engine could be very popular in the San Francisco area, but have very little data on the East Coast. This would not be a very practical approach to an online business directory.

The other source of data that these major directories use is directly from the consumers themselves. End users want to add their business to an online directory to increase its visibility online, which in turn creates more business for them. So they submit their relevant business information in the hopes of getting more customers, and the website gets (theoretically) accurate information that is difficult to obtain otherwise.

This idea of "crowd sourcing" updates is becoming more and more common and has a lot of positive uses. The United States uses "crowd sourcing" to elect its officials, and we call it "voting". Companies use anonymous GPS data from phone operating systems to get real time traffic updates by measuring the speed of phones travelling on roads to get an indication of current traffic.[xviii] There are plenty of good uses for crowd sourcing. There are also problems with crowd sourcing, because it can become very difficult to discern good data from the bad.

Google currently has two main forms of crowdsourcing for its maps products. Google "My Business" is the main portal for business owners to manage their business listings and corresponding advertising, The "Map Maker" product, on the other hand, is not solely for business data, but for roads, parks, buildings and anything else that would be on a typical map (without having to fold it nineteen times to fit it in your glove compartment). Google account holders can login to the My Business portal and submit their business data, which prompts for verification. Once a business is "verified", that business is then given the right to update its information.

Businesses do move from time to time, and furniture stores appear to constantly be "losing their lease". (Maybe put your lease in a safe.) Google account holders can also log into the Mapmaker product and make edits to areas of the world with which they are familiar. Perhaps updating the map to reflect a new road, building, or to fix a typo. Had we had this feature circa 1492, perhaps we wouldn't call indigenous North Americans "Indians".[25] Business data can be submitted here as well. From people other than the business owner. And here the problem begins.

> "Google's idea is that they can only keep their maps current if they let people contribute content to that process,"

> -Mike Blumenthal, editor of Blumenthals.com in an interview with Matt Markovich of KOMO 4 news in Seattle in 2014.[xix]

---

[25]Or bad baseball teams from Cleveland.

This is a great idea in theory. Let the world police itself and the useful truth will emerge. It works every time, except when it doesn't. The problem is like the problem with so many great theoretical ideas; assholes. In this case, there are people who profit in various ways from submitting inaccurate information through these methods, and who are exceptionally good at it. The data providers don't talk about the methods they employ to fight the scammers who are posting fake business data.

This makes a lot of sense; revealing their methods would make it much easier for the criminals to be successful. But it also keeps everyone outside of these companies in the dark about what is actually being done to solve the problem. And when the problem isn't being solved, it makes us people outside the companies frustrated.

What many people have concluded is that the search engines are not doing nearly enough in the fight against fake business listings, and their willful inaction is hurting consumers and businesses all across the country.

How websites stack up

I wanted to know more about how each of the top mapping sites stacked up against each other. So I reviewed a lot of live mapping data from the various providers. This process took a lot of time, as I checked data in multiple categories, cities across all the major providers, as well as searched for individual fake businesses across all platforms. Once I had good reason to believe that a certain business listing was fake, I would check local government databases to see if they were licensed and lawfully incorporated. If they weren't, I concluded that they were "fake". Only then would a business be identified as fake, and the rating would then get applied in my scoring system. It's not infallible, so don't sue me claiming that I said it is, but it's at least one man's researched inquiry for your reading pleasure. Here are the overall results:

Google Maps

Site Name: Google Maps – http://maps.google.com. Mobile app is the "Google Maps" application on Android, iPhone and Windows phones. Consistently the highest used map and local search website and mobile application.

Fake Listings: Severe

I rated Google Maps as having a severe problem with fake listings. This means that for dozens of categories and throughout the entire country, there are hundreds of thousands of seemingly fake businesses that are operating on Google Maps and consistently ranking in the top 10 for their keyword searches.

Fake Reviews: Severe

As with the fake listings, there are also epidemic levels of fake reviews that go along with the fake listings. The people behind the building of the fake businesses get careless and leave a very easy trail to other fake listings. They boost the rankings of their fake businesses with fake reviews. It is wrong to falsify reviews of your own business, whether that business is legitimate or not.

Verification of Business Data:

Google initially verifies new business data via a postcard that contains a pin number. The postcard gets mailed to the address that is specified, and the business owner can then input the code into the verification field of the Google My Business control panel. Once the code is entered, the business will then be displayed on Google Maps.

Once the data is in Google Maps, phone verification can be used to verify the business.

Both of these methods have flaws, and are consistently abused by criminals, with full knowledge of Google Maps management and employees.

Data Sharing:

Google displays data that is submitted to their site by Google users, as well as displaying data from other websites that they have sharing agreements with. This is a well-known and popular practice for websites, but can be problematic when Google does not very the data before posting it.

Customer Service: Help Forums

The Help forums are poorly staffed, and typically business owners don't get the results that they are looking for. No phone number, email or dedicated support of any kind for businesses or end users.

Site Grade: F

Overall Synapsis:

As a business owner or consumer, you can't really get around using either Google or Apple for your navigation or basic searches. You either have an Android or Apple based phone, and they come with the apps that allow you to choose either one.

Google has tried to make a lot of improvements, but still seems to be missing the mark. If you are a business owner, you simply must use Google Maps to be competitive in the marketplace. Legitimate business owners who are in one of the heavily spammed categories already know about the fraudsters who they constantly have to battle with. Consumers only get a taste of the problem when they are overcharged by a shady locksmith or other online con artist.

Bing Places

Site Name: Bing Maps https://www.bing.com/maps/

Fake Listings: Severe

Bing is new to the maps game, having entered the market well after Yelp, Google and other providers of business data. I initially thought Bing wouldn't have been as problematic, but after checking certain categories, there are often fake listings in nearly all of the top 10 spots, with no licensed businesses to be found. This is not just one isolated city or business category, but many of the top 30 cities and 40+ industries.

Fake Reviews: Severe

Fake reviews are simple to create and valuable to businesses; real and fake alike. Trust the reviews you read on Bing at your peril.

Verification of Business Data:

Bing allows you to add a business through their portal, and they allow either address verification or domain name verification. This is where they either send you a post card to verify your mailing address or verify your business domain name (such as seelysecurity.com) by sending you an email. These checks will only stop the laziest potential scammers; not anyone who does this on a large scale.

They also allow phone verifications for existing businesses that desire to update their data.

Data Sharing:

Bing appears to share data as well, as many of the large providers do. Again, this is a problem due to the lack of checks between data partners.

Customer Service: Customer service exists, but barely.

Site Grade: F

Overall Synapsis:

Don't use Bing Maps. Like most of the competition, they seem to have no one checking authenticity of the businesses they allow on their platform, and no one seems to be paying attention at all.

Using Bing Maps is almost a guarantee that you are going to get fake business results, as the only people submitting things actively are scammers.

In my opinion, it is dangerous for consumers to use Bing Maps for any local business search in any city in the United States.

Yelp

Site Name: Yelp.com

Fake Listings: Low

Of all the top tier websites that provide local business data, Yelp had the lowest amounts of seemingly fake listings in comparison to the rest. I believe it has to do a lot with their policy on data sharing and content syndication, as they don't blindly accept business data from Google and others. If they are sharing, the amount is minimal, or they have better cross-checking functionality. Either way, something is going right here.

Fake Reviews: Moderate

Yelp is one of the top brands in the local business data game, which on one hand gives them a lot of user trust, but also paints a target on them for those who would manipulate rankings and reviews. There have been recent stories about companies who posted fake reviews for a fee and were caught[xx] .

This is not Yelp's fault, and Yelp had made their internal controls so strict that to get fake reviews to stick required quite a lot of effort and luck. What's great to see is that they are continually trying to improve their detection rates and provide only legitimate reviews. It takes continuous effort, but the result is a trusted site. Consumers know and appreciate the difference.

Verification of Business Data:

Yelp has internal teams that check data, and allows business owners to claim their listings with a phone call from Yelp.

Data Sharing:

Based on my research, Yelp appears to have the most accurate data sampling of any of the top 50 most popular sites on the web. As I said earlier, I believe it is because they are not trusting syndicated data as much, or they are doing something extra to validate it.

Customer Service:

One of the only sites with easy to use help and FAQ page, as well as a support phone number, clearly posted for all users to call for help.

Site Grade: A-

Yelp is the clear winner in these rankings, and other companies would be wise to follow their lead. For those of us who studied and analyzed the data, Yelp provides the safest experience for consumers and the likelihood of being scammed by a vendor there are extremely low. \

Overall Synapsis:

When I don't have much time, and want to find more accurate business data, I use Yelp. Until the other search engines decide to clean things up, there isn't a single other search engine I would recommend using.

Angieslist.com

Site Name: Angieslist.com

Fake Listings: High

Angie's List is a difficult site to check, as you have to sign up for an account and pay a monthly fee to be able to even view search results. You can find things via a direct web search, which is how I discovered a pretty disappointing trend. They are definitely part of a group of companies that legally syndicates and shares data, but the data they are posting is often full of fake listings from other websites. I found numerous businesses they display all throughout their site that are completely bogus. Angieslist says on www.angieslist.com that "only highly rated companies can offer services through Angie's List", which appears to not be entirely accurate.

Fake Reviews: Low

Based on what I was able to see throughout their directory, the amount of fake reviews "appears" to be relatively low. Scammers have been known to be relatively smart and clever when it comes down to making money, so I wouldn't put it past them to have figured it out. When there are large numbers of fake businesses on a site, there are typically fake reviews as well.

Verification of Business Data:

Angieslist allows you to submit your business to their site with no verification via phone or address.

Data Sharing :

Angieslist shares and syndicates data with third parties, as I have found evidence in countless places. What is on Angieslist is not unique to them.

Customer Service: Excellent customer service.

Site Grade: D-

Overall Synapsis: There are worse places, but there are also better ones. And freer ones. I personally don't trust Angieslist whatsoever. They make it hard to check data across the entire country by limiting your search to one area, and make you pay for access. The consumer gets the feeling that they are part of some exclusive club that has hand picked vendors and service providers, when in fact, they are not vetting or checking credentials at all.

I won't use Angieslist under any circumstance.

WhitePages

Site Name: WhitePages.com

Fake Listings: Severe

It's bad. Numerous categories, numerous cities, with entire top 50 results that appear to be fake businesses. The chances of finding a real business in the top ten search is virtually 0 in many cases.

Fake Reviews: Severe

Any resemblance between a whitepages.com review and an actual consumer experience is purely coincidental.

Verification of Business Data:

As far as I can tell, they don't care to verify anything. Or they're super bad at it.

Data Sharing: Come one, come all, it seems.

Customer Service:

Online support portal where you can find answers to your questions, but no clearly posted chat or phone support.

Site Grade: F

Overall Synapsis: I even considered "G" for whitepages.com.

Superpages

Site Name: Superpages.com

Fake Listings: Severe

SuperPages is a hugely popular site, which is actually a part of supermedia.com, which is owned by DexMedia. Post as many as you like, as they likely won't be removed.

Fake Reviews: Severe

SuperPages allows you to post reviews of businesses anonymously, with no sign in necessary at all. It's like fan fiction for customer experiences.

Verification of Business Data

As far as I can tell, they don't care to verify anything.

Data Sharing

In all likelihood, they will accept or post any data they receive without checks for data integrity of any kind.

Customer Service

Online support portal where you can find answers to your questions, but no clearly posted chat or phone support. Not likely available.

Site Grade: F

At least their name is super.

Summary

If you care about the identity of the people entering your home to perform repairs, or want to give your money to hard working American small business owners, then note the above reviews with care.

> Parker Thompson of Leviathan Security said in an interview with KOMO in Seattle: "Google is going to end up making a decision on this, if it's in their monetary interests to do so[xxi]"

I say that it's time for the crowd to provide some feedback. It is time for the crowd to let these websites know that this is unacceptable, and start voting with our keyboards and our wallets. We must start rewarding the companies that take this problem seriously, not only on principle, but for our own safety as well.

The same article mentioned that they had forwarded the various techniques and methods that I used to build fake listings that we showed Google during a phone call the day before the story aired. Over a year later, the same methods still worked. These search companies don't appear to be taking the problem seriously at all and seem not to want to make any of the changes that would help consumers or small business owners. If they're not on the side of the general public, whose side are they on[26]?

---

[26]They're for profit corporations, dummy. They're on the side of their shareholders.

Five

Maps Fraud Explained

Now that you know that there is a problem and who is a part of it, let's talk about what happens when the search engine companies get presented with that information. You might think at first blush that they would immediately strive to rid their virtual domain of fraud, filth, dishonesty, and all other improprieties of any kind. Then you might remember that this is Earth, not Candyland, and ask yourself what course of action is in their best interests.

I have to admit, I was living in Candyland for a long time on this issue, and part of me still is. I mean, how can these companies just ignore the overwhelming evidence and media coverage of these issues? I thought there had to be a mistake. If someone just pointed things out clearly, solutions would quickly follow. After all, Google's motto is "don't be evil".

My entrance into maps fraud was in 2009, when I first found out that my employer was closing its southern California office. Having a family to support, I was open to pretty much any job. The first job I was offered was what was described to me as a "data entry" position. It turns out the gig was helping put business locations online from a pre-populated spreadsheet filled with business names, addresses, phone numbers and websites. In English: maps fraud.

At the time, it was simply a matter of doing things that I was readily capable of doing for compensation of which I had an immediate need. Since I had no prior knowledge of this area, I had no sense that anyone might be getting hurt by what I was doing. Due to lax security and verification requirements, it was exceedingly easy to get the businesses to verify. Back then, you could verify a brand new business with just a phone call, and presto, it was live. Once that changed, I was tasked with finding ways around the postal verification or otherwise staying one step ahead of the search engine companies. It wasn't difficult.

The first trick that I came up with was ordering multiple postcards to the same address with different suite numbers. For example,

Bryan's Burritos
1600 E 6th St Suite 101
Seattle, WA 98109

and

Bryan's Taco's
1600 E 6th St Suite 102
Seattle, WA 98109.

What I ended up finding was that you could easily get upwards of 500 postcards all shipped to the same address, and the websites wouldn't know the difference. Now, there are obvious drawbacks to having 500 business locations at the same address (especially in the same business type). But good news, fans of evil! Once you have a business verified with a postcard, you can use a secondary account to claim that business listing and move it anywhere in the country you want. That trick is detailed in the next chapter, and it still works. Yes, 6-7 years later, the loophole that has proved to be the most useful for scammers is still wide open.[27]

I was good at my job, and there is something about success in any endeavor that feels good. But the better I got at my work, the more discontent I became. By the time I was tasked with the planning and building of fake listings, there was no denying the magnitude and impact of what we were doing. We had built over 3000 fake businesses in just one category (automotive service related business) and our boss was wildly successful. I felt terrible. It was awful knowing that what we were doing was ultimately lying to consumers and that the entire industry around it was just a lie. I didn't feel good about what I was doing, I wasn't gaining any experience I could carry into legitimate business, and our sole purpose was to be one step ahead of the companies trying to stop spam. I started looking for other work related to IT services,

---

[27]Unless it isn't anymore. Here's hoping.

networking and consulting. When I found other work, I left. My soul was replenished.

A couple years later, I began to wonder if the search engines ever got their act together and I started checking out my old stamping grounds again. What I ended up finding was that not only was spam still alive and well, but the scammers were more active and successful than ever before. There were still tons of ways that people were abusing the system, and the overall count on spam was much higher in every business category that I checked.

Enough was enough. It was time to tell Google and the other sites what problems they were having and how exactly scammers were getting it done. So in late 2013, I started submitting methods for how to hack Google Maps directly to Google via security@google.com.

Google's Response
February 3rd 2014

Thanks for the vulnerability report. This email confirms we've received your message. We'll investigate and get back to you once we've got an update.
Cheers,
Google Security Bot

February 3rd 2014
Hey - Just letting you know that your report was triaged and we're currently looking into it. You should receive a

response in a couple of days, but it might take up to a week if we're particularly busy.
Thanks,
Google Security Team

February 7th 2014
Hey,

Thanks for your note. If you believe you have found vulnerability here, please provide detailed instructions on how to reproduce the issue. If we are able to reproduce the issue ourselves, we'll file a bug with the relevant team, and the vulnerability reward program panel will review your submission to determine if it is eligible for reward or credit. More info on the program is available here: http://www.google.com/about/appsecurity/reward-program/index.html. Thanks!

Regards,
Adam B.

February 11th 2014
Hey Bryan,

Thanks for the additional details, and apologies for my delay in getting back to you. I'm having a little trouble understanding your report - it sounds like you are creating fake business listings via Map Maker? What is the security impact of this issue? It sounds like you are finding ways to profit off of these fake business listings, but again, I'm not sure I follow the process you are describing. If you could provide more details, that would be great. I have also passed this information along internally to check-in with the relevant teams. Thanks!

Regards,
Adam B.

February 12th, 2014
Hey Bryan,

I heard back from the relevant teams internally, and it sounds like this is a spam/abuse issue. While we appreciate your diligence in reporting this issue to us, these types of issues typically do not qualify for reward or credit under the vulnerability reward program, more info on that is available here: http://www.google.com/about/appsecurity/reward-program/index.html. Thanks!

Regards,
Adam B.

That was the last email I received from Google on the subject. They were giving no reward for information, but I wasn't looking for reward. I thought that the problem needed to be addressed, but I didn't feel like they were really concerned about it.

Different Approach

So, I tried a different approach. I started creating listings on Google Maps that were obviously satirical. I did it both because I thought it was funny and because I wanted to prove my point. I didn't tell anybody and I didn't advertise it. I created several ridiculous listings over the course of a week or so. The first one was discovered by someone in the Seattle area and was then shown to Google Maps and local search expert Nyagoslav Zhekov, one of the authors on Whitespark.ca. GOOGLE MAPS STILL TOO EASY TO SPAM (post dated February 19, 2014). And as you can see in the screenshot and on his website, you'll see my not-so-subtle posting in downtown Bellevue, WA: "Lol Google u r my bit.ch".

Bellevue is a major city near the greater Seattle metropolitan area. It wouldn't be long before this would get noticed by a Jane Doe or two.

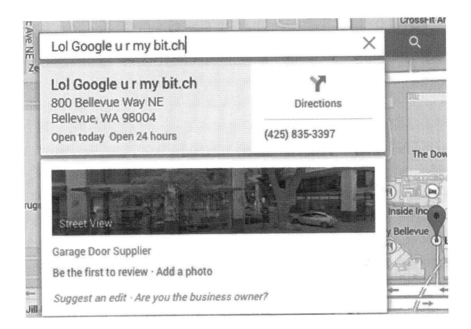

Lol Google u r my bit.ch ✕ 🔍

Lol Google u r my bit.ch
800 Bellevue Way NE
Bellevue, WA 98004
Open today Open 24 hours

Directions

(425) 835-3397

Street View

Garage Door Supplier

Be the first to review · Add a photo

Suggest an edit · Are you the business owner?

Figure 5.1

You may notice the phone number on this listing - it was my Google voice number at the time, which I was using sparingly. It's still mine, and it's also the number on SeelySecurity.com.

I had always known that the websites' refusal to do anything about the spam was a problem, and Nyagoslav and Mike Blumenthal's support (another expert on maps fraud) confirmed for me that it was big enough to get Google's attention. This time, I bypassed the "Report a Problem" button. I called the first local news channel I could think of and ended up getting in touch with veteran technology reporter Matt Markovich of KOMO 4. Matt and his cameraman showed up the next day, filmed a few things and we talked about the problem. They spent the next week or two working and they created a story called "Insider: Google 'map jacking' is rampant, a threat to public safety."

The day before it was set to air, Google reached out via phone to talk to me. One of the people on the call was a Director of Engineering. Let's call him "Bob". The other person on the call didn't say much, but I was told that she was in media relations.

I explained the process that I was using to create listings and accomplish the various pranks. Over the next twenty to thirty minutes, his only response to any of my claims was "that's not possible" or "you can't do that". He said this to quite a few of my explanations.

Considering that the story had not aired yet, Bob had not seen any of the proof. So he is either blessed with a firm skepticism or an overriding optimism. Toward the end of the call I made a pretty bold claim, which was that I could make a new business listing to show them in a major city, and rank it within the top 3 for its category in less than 15 minutes. If you were to ask any Google Maps expert what they thought about this, they would probably tell you that this was impossible as well.

What makes this claim particularly audacious is that in order to do this from scratch, one would normally have to request a postcard, wait 3-5 days, and then validate the listing with the pin number on the post card. To build a listing from scratch would take no less than 4 days. I was claiming that I could not only complete the entire process in 15 minutes, but I could also have it outrank existing businesses, complete with website, pictures, reviews and be within the top 3 for a major category, in a major city.

Ranking a new business in a small town is not very difficult, since there is virtually no competition. Ranking something in a major city, however, can take months or even years, and even then you might not get on the front page of results.

So you can imagine that Bob would have been skeptical, hence his attitude of "that's not possible" and general disagreeability. Maybe he thought I was wasting his time.

Now, if the problem was just that people are messing with maps to get a chuckle about Vladimir Putin's face on a rainbow flag, I can see why Google didn't seem to hop on my high-alert train. But as these things usually go, something that looks like a harmless loophole has the potential for becoming a national security problem. Fortunately (or unfortunately, I can't decide which), my brain sees those awful paths alongside the ridiculous and funny options.

So at the end of the call, it was time to back up my "bold claim". I explained that however funny some of the pranks were, that there were indeed awful and potentially scary implications for this loophole and said something to the effect of:

"Well, the scariest thing I could imagine at this point is dropping off my kid at a childcare center that I found on Google Maps, and not knowing if the daycare was real."

With that we ended the call, and I promptly created a fake childcare in Shoreline, Washington. I called it HOPES AND DREAMS CHILDCARE, and it ranked in the top three businesses for the city of shoreline within ten minutes (I took the listing down quickly after sending it to Google). I sent the link to Bob, and did not hear back from him or anyone else at Google since. In ten short minutes this fake childcare business had a phone number, a picture, a functioning website, two reviews and a top three ranking. Parents all over North Seattle would see this in the results if they were to search for childcare, daycare or anything related to that category.

The story broke on KOMO the next day; fake childcare listing and all. The KOMO story was thorough, but it didn't generate a huge buzz or any follow-up questions from other outlets. I started thinking about what else I could do with this loophole. The answer staggered me.

Since you can think about these kinds of things anywhere, I went to McDonald's. Don't you go there to think about how to break things on the Internet? While my daughter was tearing up the play area as she does, I started tinkering around on the Wi-Fi as I do, and ended up coming up with an idea that took things much further than anyone thought possible.

How I got on all of the lists

Instead of pursuing profit with fake businesses, or messing with listings for giggles (I do love a good giggle), what if you focus on information? Real information, especially secret information, is more powerful to some people than money.

Who has interesting information? Probably a lot of people, but I put my money on the Federal Bureau of Investigation and the Secret Service. But how do you get information from the FBI through Google Maps?

Well, it turns out that you can call branches of the federal government just like you can call a locksmith. And often with the same degree of urgency. They're listed on Google Maps and the other local directory sites. In a fit of inspiration and/or insanity, I created a Secret Service listing in Washington, D.C., an FBI listing in San Francisco and arranged them directly on top of the existing public listings. I copied all the pictures from the original businesses and made them look identical. But the two originals still ranked number one and my fake proof-of-concept listings ranked number two. The only thing that was different was that the Secret Service and FBI listings actually had "customer reviews" on them.

So in order to make mine outrank the real locations, I had to add reviews to the fake ones, and delete real reviews from the real locations. Anyone can go look at public reviews, but there isn't a convenient little "delete" button on reviews. But you can flag reviews as "spam" and if you do this from a couple of accounts from different IP addresses, Google's automated system will say "ok, these are spam," and remove the positive reviews.

The reviews I put on the fake listings boosted up the rankings immediately, and once the real reviews were removed, the ranking of the listings switched. Now my fake listings were ranking #1 and the real locations were ranked #2.

Now the phone numbers that were on these listings were purchased online from a website that typically caters to businesses that either want toll free or local numbers for franchises or marketing purposes. Many of these companies will use a unique toll free or local number for specific commercials, as a means of tracking which advertisement is performing better. For instance, if you had a commercial on channel 5 at noon and channel 6 at noon, how will you determine which does better if you use the same phone number? If you use two numbers and route the calls from each number to your main customer service number, you can then accurately measure responses, as well as implement features such as call recording, hunt groups or other calling features. The call recording feature is very common, and as consumers, we typically hear a voice saying, "your call may be recorded for quality assurance purposes". This warning is a feature of these services that allows companies to use the call recordings; otherwise, recording your call without consent can be against the law in most places.

When I built the listings, I was faced with two options. I could route the calls to my cell phone and play it straight to see what I could get the caller to divulge. Or, I could treat these calls as "leads", and automatically forward them to the actual federal locations. I suppose I could have answered the phone "This is Agent Mulder" and laughed hysterically. But that would have been lame even when that reference was timely.

Within a couple of hours after the business listings were created and finalized for my Secret Service & FBI tests, calls started to come in. When the first call came in, the system was devised to email me a message letting me know that a call came through. Up until this point, I had assumed it would work, but there was still the uncertainty and work to be done while preparing. Once that email came though, everything changed. It felt like time stood still for a second.

I think anyone who grew up around computers and technology in the last 20 years would have the same overall understanding of the gravity of what just happened. We all know that recording phone calls without the other person's permission is generally not legal, but this can vary state to state. However I don't believe there are any states that allow a third party to record two other people having a private phone call. Taking that even further is recording federal agents having a private conversation.

The only way that the circumstances could have been worse would be if they happened to be talking about actual classified information or if the person was a Senator, Congressman or a Sagittarius. I had thought about taking it to that extreme, but once this proof-of-concept was successful, it was pretty clear to me that this would be enough to get people's attention.

I distinctly remember thinking "Crap! I have to tell somebody." To be quite honest, I had not really thought the whole disclosure part through. Once the calls started coming in, that was it: I had to tell someone right away. An argument could be made that this could be used for financial gain, considering most of this book talks about that aspect. The other malicious purpose would be for information gathering. The NSA's very existence proves that information can be valuable to some.

Figure 5.2

This figure shows the real Secret Service location in results spot A, and the fake location in spot B. As you can see, the reviews total is 2, vs. the second listing having only 1.

Figure 5.3

This figure shows the real FBI location in A, with the fake location in B. Notice the 425 area code in spot B "should" be a dead giveaway. But it's not.

This was either the smartest thing I've ever done or the dumbest thing I've ever done. I am still trying to figure out which. Using maps fraud to record federal law enforcement agents with neither party's awareness is an ill-advised activity. You absolutely, positively, should not try it. If you do, you will get caught and go to prison. I was a journalist doing it for specific journalistic purposes without any criminal intent...and I still feel fortunate that I haven't been run through years of court battles to eat my meals not on trays.

I'm not an attorney, but the common sense I do possess told me that at best I'd be frowned upon. At worst, I imagined that I might be misunderstood right into Guantanamo Bay. But as I am who I am, I found myself without an instruction manual on what to do with one of the FBI's calls you recorded that you shouldn't have ever heard. To be fair, if there was a manual for what to do in that very specific situation, I probably wouldn't have read it yet, but that's beside the point.

The next morning, I called a friend who works in the FBI and told him what I did. This took a while because it's not exactly easy to explain when the person isn't familiar with the Google Maps loopholes. When I finally managed to get it into his head, he recommended that I call the local FBI office branch, explain, and await further instructions. Within the first 24 hours, there were dozens of calls that had come through to the Secret Service office and FBI office through these fake listings. I had listened to a couple of them and realized that I didn't want to listen to any more in case I heard something that one cannot un-hear, like government secrets or country music.

Imagine my call to my friendly neighborhood FBI.

Hello, I intercepted calls to the Secret Service and the FBI in San Francisco, by doing A, B, and C.

Yeah, uh-huh. All right. Well, what would you like us to do?

Well, I'd like to come in and actually show you guys, because this is a problem.

Right, well, we'll have someone get back to you.

I gave him my number, hung up and, after a few hours passed, there was still no call. I assumed they would not be calling. They probably didn't believe me. The guy was probably laughing his butt off after my call. He probably thought I was wearing a tinfoil hat and preparing for the end times. It makes me wonder how many other calls they get from crazy people going, "You know what? I think my mailman is an alien and he's stealing all of our chocolate milk." Like, what kind of crazy crap do people report? The trouble is, I really had recorded their calls and really did think this was an issue worth their time. Besides, you can always get more chocolate milk.

The Secret Service

Figure 5.4 -

This figure shows what I saw when I walked in to report what I had found. Seemed like as good a time as any to take a selfie.

Like any loyal American would do, I packed my laptop and drove down to the Secret Service office in downtown Seattle. In their tiny lobby I explained why I was there. The eye rolling was incredible. Despite the fact that my use of Edward Snowden's name in my ridiculous White House Lawn listing in the news story two days prior probably landed me on some list somewhere of people to watch, they still didn't believe me. Special Agent "Tom" showed up, and he didn't believe me either.

I pulled my laptop out, hooked it up to my phone, connected to the control panel for my special forwarding service and asked them to call the D.C. office right then, to finally prove that I could do what I was claiming. The agent agreed, pulled out his smart phone, and began his search to humor me.

This was a pivotal moment. I was gambling everything on the fact that he would search for the D.C. Secret Service via the Google Maps App. I hadn't thought ahead enough to get these fake listings also published on any other maps services. It had to be Google Maps. Especially since we were standing in this very tiny lobby with several other very skeptical agents, all with the same eye rolling problem.

I would have looked pretty dumb after the call was over if he called the correct number directly and I had just wasted their time. Correction: I would have looked even dumber than the guy who had just recorded the Secret Service, walked into their office, and told them voluntarily. That guy was a total idiot.

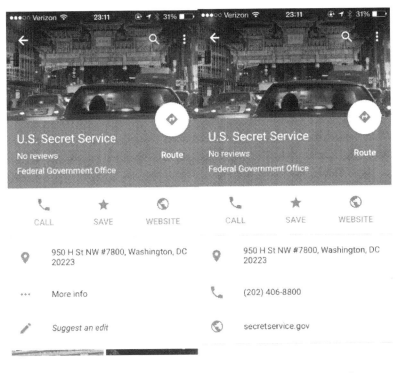

Figure 5.5   *Figure 5.6*

The Google Maps App on your phone makes my loophole even easier than on the web. Business listings show addresses and an icon that will call the number listed on the page when you tap it. It doesn't show the phone number because it's too much text. To reveal the phone number, you tap on the words "More info" (Figure 5.6.)

An out of state phone number would be suspicious on any listing; enough to make skeptical and savvy users think twice. If you don't see it, and instead trust your product to have correct information, you'll skip checking the number and miss the fact that a Washington State number is listed for a Washington D.C. business location.

So this agent proceeded to talk to the guy in the Secret Service office in D.C. for a few minutes. Just a few, very long minutes. He hung up.

My phone buzzed.

It was a text message that read:

> You have received a call from '206-xxx-xxxx' inbound to your campaign named 'Secret Service Office Washington DC'

I went to the recent calls in my laptop call manager.

I pressed play and we heard Agent Tom on this side talking and then we heard the other agent talking. That is when Agent Tom said the two key words I had been waiting to hear:

"Oh shit."

All of the eyeballs in the room stopped rolling. The skeptical agents experienced an abrupt attitude change.

Now, history has proven that humans traditionally take one particular stand towards things that are new, different, or controversial. I wish that that stance were dialogue and reasonable debate. More often than not it is, in essence, "AHHHH, kill it with fire".

So when their eyes snapped back into place, I was hoping for a chance to talk things out before facing a scene from a Monty Python movie which ends with me being burned alive for witchcraft due to my mass equaling that of an arbitrary waterfowl.

Cue the full pat down, bag search, and acknowledgement of my Miranda Rights. Now I was being very strongly encouraged to come with them into the "guest suite." Did I say guest suite? I mean interrogation room. They said I was not being detained, and I was not under arrest, but there is something about having a door shut behind you that lends a certain finality to this kind of situation. There was no turning back now. I wondered how long it would take them to decide what they would be doing with me.

I might be an idiot, but I am not a complete idiot. Prior to walking into the federal building, I made sure that people knew that I was doing this and why. I called three friends who are Seattle cops, two news agencies, one FBI agent friend, and a partridge in a pear tree.

I am not saying that I truly believed that the Secret Service was going to shoot me and dump my body in a river. The nearest river was pretty far away and carrying a burlap sack that weighs 240 pounds is not an easy task. Driving all the way to a river to dump my body would be a complete waste of taxpayer dollars. Not to mention that the Suburban's CO_2 emissions on that long trip would be pretty outrageous. Seattleites like to be green when they can be. But let's just say that the notion that my life would be irrevocably changed for the worse weighed heavily and sincerely on my mind.

The guest suite was not very exciting. From my uncomfortable plastic chair across the table from Agent Tom, I noted the nearby handcuff bar. Definitely no turning back now.

Yet another agent came in.

"All right, so you really did what you told us you did."

They set down a printed article of the KOMO news story from earlier that week.

"This is you."

"Yeah. I've been trying to tell you guys there's a problem."

"We believe you now. How the hell did you do this?"

For the next few hours, I walked them through the process of creating a fake Google Maps listing from scratch. I then created two more fake listings on my laptop in front of three Secret Service agents.

If you're ever at the Secret Service with your laptop, I recommend bringing a smartphone specifically so you can create your own personal hotspot. Who knew the Secret Service didn't offer complimentary wifi to their guests?[28]

Agents came in and out as I repeated the process numerous times to explain myself.

"No, I did not break into the Secret Service's phone system. No, I didn't hack into any Secret Service computers."

They were understandably confused. I get that a lot. Eventually the Special Agent in charge of the Seattle office said he was on the phone with someone at Google who was demanding answers. I believe him, though THAT is the call I would have LOVED to have intercepted. Can you imagine being the guy on the other end? The Secret Service calls because they are not happy with your company. You don't have answers and they are demanding something.

Even now, I giggle thinking about what could have been said on the other end of that line. I couldn't imagine that the strategy they tried on me -- which was basically the Obi-Wan Kenobi trick of waving your hand and hoping it erases the other person's memory -- would work on the people charged with protecting the President. But I'll never know.

Eventually, the Agent in charge came back in to tell me to delete all of the listings I created for them, including the FBI and Secret

---

[28]Fricking Obama.

Service. With three agents looking over my shoulder, I was stuck in boredom for another 30-45 minutes until things got even weirder.

They said I was a hero.

I generally associate the word "hero" with firefighters and Superman.[29] Considering I am neither of those, I was now the confused one in the room. I had taken a process that I had previously used to scam people, got bored with it, and figured out something potentially more dangerous to do with it. Instead of having criminal intent and then walking into the Secret Service, I considered the national security implications and had to tell someone. No criminal intent meant I walked out of the Secret Service under my own power instead of learning how hard it is to breathe underwater while inside of a large burlap sack. Not to mention how itchy that would be.

With this grateful breath in my lungs, I called Nitasha Tiku at Gawker. She started writing the story and it was published within days. It was called How a Hacker Intercepted FBI & Secret Service Calls With Google Maps.[xxii]

My LinkedIn profile went from 1-2 views a week to hundreds. Kevin Mitnick, famed hacker and one of my security idols, followed me on Twitter. It was insane.

Gizmodo - It's Ridiculously Easy To Troll Google Maps with Fake Listings, by Eric Limer (Trust the listings you

---

[29]Not affiliated with Superpages.com.

find on Google Maps? You shouldn't, because it's dumb easy to fake them.)[xxiii]

Bloomberg HOW SCAMMERS TURN GOOGLE MAPS INTO FANTASY LAND by Dune Lawrence[xxiv]

KOMO News MAN USED GOOGLE FLAW TO EAVESDROP ON CALLS TO SECRET SERVICE by Matt Markovich[xxv]

San Francisco Bay Guardian HACKER PRANKS SAN FRANCISCO FBI USING GOOGLE MAPS EXPLOIT by Joe Fitzgerald Rodriguez[xxvi]

My least favorite part of the story is the death threats I received from people who, I can only assume, are mad that I've revealed secrets about the loophole they are exploiting for money. Nitasha Tiku said she received death threats around that time as well. There were even posts on "SEO" forums that said something to the effect of "If you were screwed over by Bryan Seely and his disclosure of this information, message me, we are going to make sure that this asshole gets what's coming to him."

When I first received the threats, my immediate concern turned to my children. I was not terribly worried for my own safety, but for theirs. I reported the text messages and forum posts to the U.S. Secret Service and saw the post removed from the forum fairly quickly, and never received another message again. I am grateful to the Secret Service for handling it the way that they did. People who whine about our government have no idea how hard it is to do what they do or how much worse things could be.

Truthfully, I knew that people would be mad about my disclosure. This is a huge moneymaker for many people. I used to be one of them. So many legitimate business owners don't even know how or why they're losing business. It's wrong to make money this way and if this book can help to cut the production of these fake listings, the world will be a better place.

Google's Response

So what did Google have to say about all of this? Here is the initial response from a Google spokeswoman to KOMO 4 Seattle.

> "It was brought to our attention that an individual was creating fake business listings in Google Maps. Although these listings do not appear prominently on the map, we take problems like spam very seriously, and appreciate when the community flags issues so we can quickly resolve them."

This appears to be a reference to the funny listings that were discovered by random people all over the country, and reported to the top bloggers in the Google Maps world. It is hard to imagine how being the top search result for "Secret Service" is "not prominently displayed", unless you're claiming that such a search is only a tiny percentage of the searches a person could make.

It was "prominently displayed" enough to fool the actual Secret Service. Also, since one could try to argue that this is a geographic thing, the agent in Seattle conducted the search for the listing from his phone in the Seattle office, for a location on the other side of the country. The people on the calls who were also recorded were local to the Washington D.C. area, so the results were consistent regardless of geographic location.

The Secret Service has expertise in spotting fakes, and investigating counterfeit currency is part of its mission. Citizens and law enforcement agents alike found these counterfeit listings as part of their normal usage of Google Maps. So let's just say that I found this response less than fully transparent.

Another statement Google released to Bloomberg Business Week stated:

> "We work hard to remove listings that are reported to violate our policies as quickly as possible, and to check bad actors that try to game the system by altering business descriptions once they are live on Google Maps. We encourage users to let us know when they see something that might violate our guidelines by using our 'Report a Problem' tool, found at the bottom right corner of the map."

The Bloomberg Business Week article went on to say:

> Google has disabled instant phone verification, but you can still set up a business listing using the U.S. Postal Service to get your PIN. That leaves plenty of loopholes, Seely says.

Google says they are fighting spam. The results and facts are very clearly pointing to the fact that they don't take the problem seriously, and the "spam fighting" tactics they use are less effectual than they could be. This seems like a strong statement, but let me highlight again Google's stance on fighting spam:

"We encourage users to let us know when they see something that might violate our guidelines by using our 'Report a Problem' tool, found at the bottom right corner of the map."

But at that time, the "Report a Problem" tool only worked for businesses that chose to reveal their identities publicly. The fraudulent businesses we have been talking about are the ones that hide their addresses, and that fly under the radar since locksmiths, landscapers, and cleaners don't need you to find their addresses to get your business.

Since scammers hide their addresses, the "Report a Problem" tool would not work to report them. The link just went to a dead page. Unfortunately, this also meant that legitimate business owners are open to an additional vulnerability. When real business owners use their addresses to create legitimacy, the scammers can report their business in an effort to get them removed from Google rankings. They can abuse the very tool that is supposedly there to stop them.

The "Report a Problem" tool link had this flaw in March 2014. As of this publication, it still does. I will go into more depth in a later chapter regarding this particular flaw. The reason that I bring it up is that the only constructive suggestion that I heard Google offer was a recommendation that was broken and which many people in the SEO community felt was disingenuous.

Hopefully Google has fixed this problem by the time you read these pages, and I am the one who looks foolish. In that case, a great wrong will have been corrected and you will just have to take my word for how crazy the world used to be. Like when your grandparents tell you about black people used to be kept away from the polls. (Oh wait, that still happens today.) So like a better example.

But at the time of these statements, the solution they proposed did not work in a multitude of cases. I don't know if the person making the statements didn't really understand the problem, if they chose their words poorly, or if they were deliberately trying to mislead the public. I know which one I think it is, but my lawyers don't want me to tell you.

My lawyers will let me say that if a company told you to call a 1-800 number to report complaints, and that phone number was always busy, you wouldn't feel like they took your complaints very seriously.

The Secret Service instructed Google to shut off whatever it was that allowed me to do what I did. Google did…for six glorious weeks. They tweaked a few features in MapMaker and disabled phone verifications, and then re-enabled phone verifications on April 1, 2014. (Alas, the news was not an April Fool's joke.) They told the Secret Service that they would fix things. I was there, in the office, when the Special Agent in charge called and he told me, in a room full of other agents, that they told Google to shut it off until it was fixed.

But when they turned it back on, it wasn't fixed. As of this publication, it's not significantly better than it was a year prior. Google told them it would be fixed, but it was not fixed. I wonder how the Secret Service feels about its requests being ignored. It also makes me wonder which institution is currently more powerful; the United States government or Google. Personally, I think it is the government. It just needs our help to fully empower it to stop this problem, no matter what obstacles anyone who benefits from the status quo puts in the path of justice.

Six

Problems & Solutions

"It's a bad plan. What's your plan?" --Jon Snow, Game of
Thrones

It is far easier to ascribe blame for a problem than it is solve one. And for a problem that appears to be dizzyingly complex, it is natural to assume that the solution must also be so. I do not believe that this is the case. Many complicated problems can be greatly remedied by simple steps, taken with diligence.

This chapter will review the various problems in the book and propose solutions. The fact that many of these solutions have not been implemented is one of those head-scratcher type situations. Some of them are so obvious that many of you reading this book (or writing it) will wonder why they were not implemented a long time ago. Like the seat belts not having to be installed in cars until 1968, and the first laws requiring their use not being enacted until 1984. Most of the solutions presented here are not even terribly difficult. The companies in question have billions of dollars at their disposal, and many people working for them that are far more intelligent than I. So it begs the question, why aren't they doing everything they can to fix the problems? Do they care about the consumers or not? The answer is simple, if mildly frustrating: they care no more, and no less, than they required to care by the law, the marketplace, or some combination thereof. It's not fair to allocate this entire burden on the businesses and consumers who are victimized. Though it will cost them some of their massive profits, the search engines can and should do their part. Call it a tax, call it charity; just call it soon.

Solution 1

Discontinue Phone Verifications: Businesses on the search sites typically verify a business phone number as a means of ensuring that the phone number rings to the local business that it is claiming to be representing. It is common to check businesses by having call centers call a business to verify that the person answering the phone sounds like they are answering the phone of a business rather than a personal number. If the person answering says the business name, that is usually enough to pass verification.

Phone verifications need to be de-emphasized; plain and simple. With existing technology, phone numbers can be easily bought, forwarded, and used to hide the identity of individuals. When it is so easy to switch a number when someone complains, there is no longer any reliability the verification of a phone number. You might as well verify someone with a Facebook page.

Solution 2

Limit the Use of Postal Box Addresses: Post office boxes and the private companies that offer them are a major and obvious piece of the maps fraud problem. They would also be a very simple piece to dismantle. While this will make it more expensive to list a legitimate business on a given directory, this is a vital reason why it needs to happen. Postal box centers (public and private) are hubs for businesses that want to find a loophole in the post card verification system. If one fake location can create just $100 in revenue a month, (which is easily obtainable in one day, let alone an entire month) it pays for the cost of the mailbox.

The solution is to flag all of the businesses that are registered at post office boxes. There are many different mailbox store franchises, but it would not be hard for the search engine companies to find them. This information could be shared, purchased from InfoUSA or other data repositories. The government could require them to register and then share that data free with the public. Consider it just one use of the newfound millions in tax revenue that these solutions would generate.

Regus is another company that allows a sort of post card verification system, by allowing workers to use their office space and receptionists to maintain an office infrastructure without all the headaches. This is a huge savior for the businesspeople who are typically road warriors and need a place to plug in a laptop, print documents, set up meetings or have their mail collected.

All of these companies facilitate the ability to receive a post card to verify that a business exists, when in fact there is really no way to determine whether a business is legitimate.

This screenshot shows the address 100 Andover Park West, Tukwila, WA. This is the address of a UPS Store near Tukwila, WA.

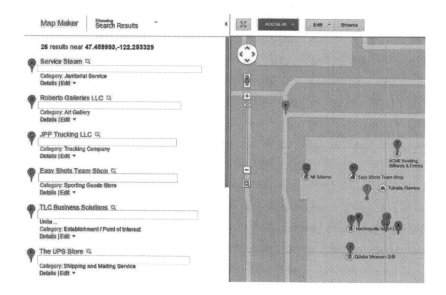

Figure 7.1

This is perfectly placed near a major transportation hub in Seattle, also near the airport. As you can see, there is a janitorial service company, a trucking company, a sporting goods store, and many other types of businesses. In some cities, there are 50-100 different companies registered at UPS stores because of how easy it is to find them. UPS stores are conscious of overlapping service areas, and they don't want to be competing with each other, so they are very well placed throughout metropolitan areas.

So many people have figured out that UPS stores could be used to game the system, that for a period of time, Google (to its credit) didn't allow businesses to register an address with the same street address as a UPS store. With your help, hopefully soon all of the search sites will implement this policy permanently. If you're a legitimate business, there needs to be a place where you can be found if you need to be sued or otherwise to answer for your actions. The Secretaries of State require such an address, so every legitimate business can simply disclose that address to the browsers if they want to come up on business searches. I truly believe that we will one day back in disbelief that there was a time when this was not how it worked.

Solution 3

Cross-Referencing other databases: All of the search companies use verification methods that are shockingly easy to falsify. Be they post card verification, telephone verification, or even laxer methods; the crooks are all five steps ahead. It's time for the "landlords"[30] to catch up.

I propose that the search companies implement a system that cross-references official government data to validate the business existing. Governments have been making such data publicly available online long enough that the search companies have numerous options

---

[30] Remember the mall analogy from the beginning? Me, too. It seems like there were more jokes back then.

from which to choose. Some companies already do this: current examples include Acxiom, Localeze, and Infousa.

The other search companies would not even have to incur a large cost to implement these types of solutions. The effect? Better data accuracy without having to incur huge cost. This would make for happier customers overall. The first of the "big boys" to do this would immediately see a spike in accuracy, and more users would follow. The rest would have to elevate their own accuracy to compete.

Remember: companies only care about consumers when compelled by either the law or the marketplace. Government verification would help the marketplace solve the problem.

Solution 4

Stricter crowdsourcing checks: The Internet loves crowdsourcing. This is not a secret. Crowdsourcing can be great when used properly, but the problem with that is that there are jerks who ruin things for everyone. There are companies that use crowdsourcing to inform the current and relevant data that they provide.

A perfect example is the Waze traffic application that allows people to report accidents, speed traps, traffic, or even police activity. The way that they limit the "jerk problem" is to limit a user's ability to report on things unless they are in the area that they are reporting. Search companies could implement the same concept on their map applications so that a user is only able to register a single location or somehow validate the identity of contributors.

These companies could be stricter with the amounts of edits new profiles are able to create, the types of things they can edit, or the amount of changes they can approve or deny. One account can submit a change, and 10 accounts can go and follow back up and approve those changes. Suddenly you have spam being published by a handful of puppet accounts.

This can be easily solved. Having to admit you made a product that can be so easily gamed is neither easy nor pleasant, but that is no reason to allow this rampant fraud to continue.

These types of checks and balances need to get implemented now. Otherwise the "crowdsourcing" platform they have built will forever be remembered as a huge travesty.[31]

Solution 5

Employee training: A byproduct of the refusal of these companies to even acknowledge that a problem exists is that they also do not train their employees to deal with the problem. Employees in Silicon Valley are the best and brightest in the world. These companies have extremely talented individuals, but if they are focused on only a narrow band of responsibility, their ability to solve problems like this is limited.

---

[31]Like the Lifetime Movie Network.

My favorite story of all time in this regard comes from a locksmith in Ohio. He emailed me and told me the following. I don't know if it's true; I'm just the messenger. But what he told me was:

"Bryan,

I own a locksmithing business in [redacted], OH and I have definitely noticed the amount of scammers in my area. I notified Google of the problem, and not only didn't the Google rep care, she had had it happen to her in Google's parking lot after work. She locked her keys in her car, call a "$15" locksmith, waited 30 minutes and got a call from someone 100 miles away who said he would send someone in 30 minutes. 2 hours later a person arrived and charged her $150 to open the car, and due to desperation, she paid it!

Google just plain doesn't care because they will take anyone's money, be they legit or a scammer, and the presence of the scammers just drives the price higher for a legitimate locksmith to compete, so for Google it's a win/win. Thanks to corporate greed, I barely pay my bills monthly."

A common problem that many companies face is that their departments have little or no security expertise. In an article I read on LinkedIn, a high level executive talked about how they liked to put security-focused engineers on other teams that typically would not have a security background. That way each product, each service, or each piece of an application has someone looking at the security implications. When you have highly complex websites like multibillion-dollar search companies, there are bound to be security problems that need to get addressed. Addressing them individually as they arise is far more efficient than ignoring them for years until major systemic reform is needed.

Companies hire ethical hackers and security consultants to test for various bugs or problems, much like how a doctor will perform allergy testing on a patient. By intentionally hacking these companies in a controlled and documented manner, the company can find the flaws, fix them and present a more complete and stable product to consumers.

When employees are focused on only their own tiny area of responsibility without regard for how hackers or criminals could misuse it, a company is doing the public a disservice. Search company employees should be given training as to the methods that are being used to circumvent their programming, as well as be allowed to collaborate and develop products that solve the problems before they start. If the engineers knew all of the different methods that these scammers were using, they would be able to build fixes immediately. But when management keeps them in the dark as to the depth and breadth of the problem, nothing changes.

If the companies want to take the fraud problem seriously, they should empower their employees to do something about it. They could train their employees that build the various pieces of their map products based on what spammers are doing, analyze the existing spam and how it was created, and put controls into place that would stop it. Consumers would immediately notice a huge difference in the amount of quality businesses versus fake businesses, and real businesses all across the country would no longer be held back by theft of valuable phone calls from consumers. The small businesses with the best services and the best reputations would rise to the top again and survival of the fittest in the capitalistic sense would be restored. With employee training, the spam problem could be reduced swiftly and business owners would get the clients they deserved in the first place.

Solution 6

Improve spam-reporting tools: This one is the thorn in the side of many people. Let's say you run a company called American Cable Company. You start getting complaints that your service is not working and affecting a large group of people. So you respond to the numerous media requests for comment and say something like:

"The alleged widespread problem of unhappy consumers is exaggerated. We encourage consumers to report any problems that they may have to USACABLE.com/ReportAProblem."

This comment gets publicly disclosed. But there are two MAJOR problems. First, the problem isn't greatly exaggerated. It's just poorly understood. Second, the link the "Report A Problem" doesn't work. It just doesn't. You'd be frustrated, wouldn't you?

That is how I feel my attempts to educate the public about maps fraud has been handled. And it frustrated me.

The phrase "alleged widespread problem" is clever lawyerspeak. When something is "alleged," it might not be true. But that doesn't mean it isn't. So the phrase can be used to distance someone from something even if they know it to be true.

The phrase "greatly exaggerated" is also clever phrasing. Exaggerated by whom? Perhaps one person, somewhere, greatly exaggerated a problem. Now the statement is true! And how could you prove it isn't? Oh, that's easy: just prove that nobody anywhere ever exaggerated the problem to a great degree. Oh, you can't? So I guess the speaker is on safe ground. Some people may greatly exaggerate the problem. But I didn't. If anything, I understated the problem. Greatly.

Then the speaker proposes two seemingly reasonable solutions for the consumer to be able to address all of their problems and make all of this silly nonsense go away. Problem solved, it would seem. Now let's get back to learning about who those Hollywood actresses are dating.[32]

The existing reporting tools simply do not work. They are links to nowhere. You know how when your computer crashes, but before it does, it asks you if you want to "report the problem"? And you know that nobody's ever going to read any such report, but maybe

---

[32] Chris Pratt. All of them are dating Chris Pratt.

for a split second you feel a tiny bit better that somewhere a microchip might care about your problem? It's like that, only some people might actually believe that someone is listening.

The existing "Report a Problem" tool does not work if a business does not report a physical address. So if the major companies adopt Solution 3 above, then "Report a Problem" could actually work. If there's someone on the other end of the "report" doing something about it.

Solution 8

Empower the public: This is a really simple approach that search companies already like to use. Crowdsourcing could be used to flag listings through the MapMaker tool, and I know that there are plenty of people who would be more than happy to spend their days flagging fake listings.

Two issues need to be addressed for this to work. Verifying that the person flagging listings is the person who they claim to be, and narrowing the scope of what they are able to flag.

If you validated the person's identity, and perhaps came up with some sort of points based rewards system that allows for some sort of appreciation, this could be a really big thing. People would be more than happy to volunteer time to help clean up the maps fraud, but currently, there is no way for them to do so. Or maybe when they pull down a fraudulent listing, it can automatically report the good deed to their Facebook feed. We can pay them in "likes".

The "report a link" tools don't work. All of us are looking at the spam and can do nothing about it. That needs to change.

Solution 9

Remove address hiding: Address hiding is another term for the feature that several major companies permit for Service Area Businesses. I can understand why they enabled this feature to begin with, since it offers small business owners the chance to be listed while simultaneously protecting the business owner's privacy. But if you have to hide your business and require a lot of privacy, then you shouldn't be running a public business. Running a business and taking money from consumers means that you are giving up some degree of privacy, and since legal businesses can be looked up in public records, this feature does nothing to protect legitimate businesses from public scrutiny. All it does is help scammers avoid detection.

This feature simply must go.

Solution 10

Fix the algorithms for fraud detection. No one outside of the individual search companies knows what the algorithms and programming that process and detect fraud looks like. My guess is that they have them in place to detect some of the more obvious forms of spam, but they don't spend enough time updating them to combat the changing techniques and methods that scammers use.

The people trying to outsmart these companies don't have to stay very far ahead; just far enough to keep their listings online. They find something that works and it's worth spending money on manpower to rapidly increase the amount of listings that go online.

These search companies have to take this more seriously. Like supermarkets staffing checkout stands, multibillion-dollar search companies would rather have a robot do a job than a human if given the choice. But if companies really want to outsmart people, they need to enlist people to do the job. Hire people to hack you, tell you how they did it, and how you could have stopped them. Then fix those problems and do it again. Stay perpetually vigilant against fraud, like companies in other industries are required to do. Industries who share the cost of fraud, rather than passing it down the line. The law isn't making you do it, so do it for a competitive advantage in the marketplace or because this book shames you into doing it. I don't care why...just do it.

Solution 11

Checking partner data: "Partner Data" is data that is shared among the largest of the mapping and directory services. This data is entered into one location, such as CitySearch.com, and then CitySearch shares that data with its "partners". Typically the data ends up on all of the other major directories. So let's say you input your business data on CitySearch. CitySearch makes money in a variety of ways, one of which is to charge customers to "spread" their information across all of the other directory services. They typically will do this for free for basic listing information, but charge for a more "premium" version of this service. The premium service typically includes pictures, reviews and data other than the basic name, address and phone number.

Small business owners are getting very savvy these days, and in order to provide customers with the most current business data, these web sites have had to get smart and figure out when to charge customers and what to provide for free.

As I talked about earlier, Moz, BrightLocal, WhiteSpark, and many other companies provide services that spread your information in the form of "citations". These are very beneficial to your business, but what happens when spam is spread in this fashion? Bad things happen.

Summary

None of these solutions are outrageous or even unreasonable. Most of them are fairly simple to execute and implement. They are simple, clear and actionable protocols that can be immediately addressed.

These companies can easily improve their products and score a major public relations victory; a win-win. Tens of thousands of small business owners, their families, customers and many consumers across the country are hurting; some of them are losing everything. Fix the problem, make it all go away, and the public will be very quick to forgive. I know I will be. Until then, the battle continues.[33]

Seven

Going After the Spammers

As brave and great generally as we all think I am, I cannot truthfully claim that I am the first person to try to bring about change in the area of maps fraud. And since I place such a high premium on the truthfulness of information, I think it best that I now highlight some (other?) heroes who have spent their time and money trying to make a difference on this issue.

Most people affected by maps fraud do not have the resources to fight a traffic ticket; let alone a billion-dollar corporation. It takes money and bravery to even try. To win, it's going to take our help.

In this chapter, we're going to talk about the different agencies, organizations, and people that have been going after the search companies and other purveyors of false commercial information. One of the recent parties who has decided to take on several companies is Mark Baldino.

Mark Baldino is a locksmith from Virginia. He runs a locksmith company called Baldino's Lock & Key in Lorton, Virginia.

Baldino's also serves customers in Maryland, Washington D.C. and the greater Virginia area. Baldino's has been open for over 40 years and was started by Mark's father, Albert. Mark started working at his father's business in 5th grade, learned the trade and once he graduated college, he returned to work full time in the family business. A more heartwarming and typically American success story is hard to imagine.

This is a business that has been built in the local community, one that has provided a valuable service to residents and that operates honestly in every respect.[34] Through good management and hard work, Baldino's grew to 15 locksmith locations (that's ACTUAL locations, with employees and everything) throughout Virginia and Maryland, and a wholesale supply distributorship that employed over 100 highly trained technicians.

Unlike many "old school" businesses, Mark had the wisdom to keep up with current trends in marketing. And that meant that Mark understood the necessity of a real and intelligent Internet presence. Web presence now is far more vital than a listing in the Yellow Pages 30 years ago. Mark has an excellent website http://www.baldinos.com/ along with his Google+ / Places listing, and his business is more than just a hobby. It is his livelihood, as well as the livelihood of his employees and their families.

---

[34]As far as I know. Don't start boosting stereos and get me sued, Mark.

Figure 8.1

The locksmith community has been one of the hardest hit by scammers, as we talked about in an earlier chapter. Legitimate locksmiths have been affected, and this is the perfect example of someone who got sick of having his business affected by maps fraud.

In 2007, he had annual sales of about $6.7 million. In 2008, he noticed sales were declining. Mark (who I have spoken to on several occasions) said it was obvious that it was search engines and these map related directories that were contributing to the decline of roughly $2 million in revenue. That's a significant drop over a few years, especially since his business was growing consistently for so long. And based on what we've already learned, it's not hard to see why Mark's business would be particularly susceptible to attack by the spammers; he's in a service industry without need of a physical location and he services a wide geographic area.

Mark did what I did. He "reported a problem" to the various search engines. He even submitted lists of fake companies directly to these companies in the hope that they would remove the fakes and things would get back to normal. He was emailing them back in 2012, and having detailed discussions about how cyber fraud was affecting his business. He told them about the flaw in the "Report a Problem" tool, and various other problems so they were very much aware of the concerns and the problems with their product as a whole. They could not claim ignorance. So they claimed indifference.

Eventually, Mark got sick of it. He sued Google, Yellow Book, Zip local, Super Media Sales, and other search engines   He filed the case in May of 2014 in United States Federal Court. I won't read you the entire complaint (because I'm not actually there; that voice in your head is really your own), but you can see the entire complaint on my website.[35] Mark alleges that all of the companies listed have the time, resources and basic technical skills required to check the validity of business listings. And he alleged that they should have to do it.

He suggested many of the solutions detailed in the previous chapter. When there is money in change, these companies are on the cutting edge of innovation. Google, for example, has spent years designing

----

[35]Remember, lawsuits contain "allegations", not proven facts. Not everything in a lawsuit is true. For example, a few years ago someone sued O.J. Simpson for "allegedly" killing some people. He was found liable for those deaths; even though we all know that O.J. was totally innocent, because he was acquitted by a jury of his fans. I mean, peers. As always, consider the source.

and building self-driving cars and worked with state governments to get them tested and legalized. But when there is uncertainty in change, and money in the status quo, corporate motivations are very different.

Another part of Baldino's complaint specifically addresses the ability to make false claims through Adwords and similar advertising.

What Baldino and many others have discovered is that the fraudulent locksmiths are advertising rates that are too good to be true.

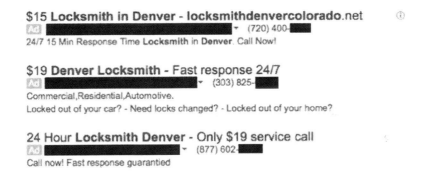

Figure 8.2

When you conduct a search for Lorton,VA locksmith, you get advertisements on the top of the main search results and on the right hand side of the search results as well.

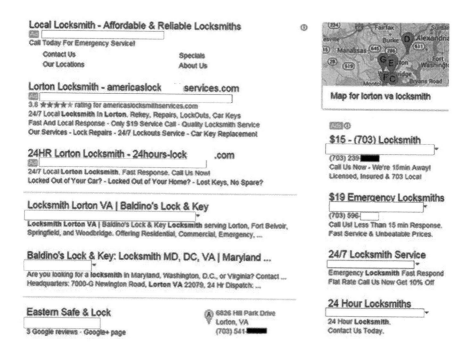

Figure 8.3

This screenshot was taken on February 17, 2015. What you see off to the right is $15 "(703) Locksmith" and $19 "Emergency Locksmiths". These two are perfect examples of the problem that Mark cites in his complaint. These businesses are advertising prices that are economically impossible. When you click or call these businesses and have them come unlock your car, or let you back into your house, they will end up charging you anywhere from $150 to $300, sometimes even more.

They know that you are desperate, or need someone immediately, and that they won't be caught. Catching these guys in the act only catches the one guy who showed up, as numerous news stories have covered across the country over the years. The problem is that the search engines are allowing them to advertise these rates with impunity.

The search engines know that these businesses are fake and that these prices are ridiculously low. They have been made aware that this practice is occurring and that the people advertising on their site are harming consumers. So what did the Defendants do? They paid lawyers lots of money[36] to understand the problems set forth in these allegations, and then make arguments to further their right NOT to correct those problems. And it worked.[37] Their ally: current federal law.

According to Wikipedia[xxvii], Section 230 of the Communications Decency Act of 1996 (also known as Title V of the Telecommunications Act of 1996):

> "[A]dded protection for online service providers and users from actions against them based on the content of third parties, stating in part that "No provider or user of an interactive computer service shall be treated as the publisher or speaker of any information provided by another information content provider".

Google's[38] own Policy says:

---

[36]Allegedly.

[37]Definitely.

[38] Just to take one random example.

Liability for our Services

WHEN PERMITTED BY LAW, GOOGLE, AND GOOGLE'S SUPPLIERS AND DISTRIBUTORS, WILL NOT BE RESPONSIBLE FOR LOST PROFITS, REVENUES, OR DATA, FINANCIAL LOSSES OR INDIRECT, SPECIAL, CONSEQUENTIAL, EXEMPLARY, OR PUNITIVE DAMAGES.

TO THE EXTENT PERMITTED BY LAW, THE TOTAL LIABILITY OF GOOGLE, AND ITS SUPPLIERS AND DISTRIBUTORS, FOR ANY CLAIMS UNDER THESE TERMS, INCLUDING FOR ANY IMPLIED WARRANTIES, IS LIMITED TO THE AMOUNT YOU PAID US TO USE THE SERVICES (OR, IF WE CHOOSE, TO SUPPLYING YOU THE SERVICES AGAIN).

IN ALL CASES, GOOGLE, AND ITS SUPPLIERS AND DISTRIBUTORS, WILL NOT BE LIABLE FOR ANY LOSS OR DAMAGE THAT IS NOT REASONABLY FORESEEABLE.

This specific section is one of the defenses that the Defendants used; arguing that they are absolutely not liable for the actions of the users on their site or anything that those users publish; no matter how certain they may be that the information being published is false and damaging.

There are several legal arguments set forth in the trial court's memorandum opinion dismissing all Defendants.[39]

But the thrust of it is this: "Defendants are immune under Section 230 of the Communications Decency Act....despite their knowledge of the false information." And the reason is the following factual assertion that currently has the force of law: "<u>Although editorial discretion might be feasible for the traditional print publisher, the sheer number of postings on interactive computer services would create an impossible burden in the Internet context</u>."

So, your local newspaper can be sued if they allow an ad for $19 locksmiths to run. But your local (international) Internet service provider can't, because of the "sheer number" of posts.

Unfortunately, the problem is not with this decision, but the current state of the law. There is potentially a valid reason for the ISP's of the world not to have an affirmative obligation to vet their postings for false information. However, Baldino's lawsuit alleges that the Defendants KNEW THAT CERTAIN LISTINGS WERE FALSE, and they <u>still</u> have no obligation to take any action with respect to them. This simply is not fair.

Let's say that I created a website called Amazing-Handymen-Seattle.com. Maybe I could get James Taylor to perform our jingle.[40]

---

[39]See United States District Court, Eastern District of Virginia, Case No. 1:14-cv-00636, filed January 27, 2015. These can't all be jokes.
[40]You're welcome for that hilarious music reference, our very oldest readers.

Then I allow handymen to register on my site and show their business profiles to consumers, and allow the handymen to advertise on the site. Consumers will hopefully come to my site to find great handymen, right? They'd come running to me. So now I can charge the handymen to advertise, and the consumers find great services.

Unfortunately, all of the handymen advertising are scamming consumers. Every last one of them. What a bummer. Frustrated customers complain to me, the owner of the site, and tell me that they are being scammed, stolen from, or defrauded by these fake handymen who show up and steal stuff from them while pretending to work.

Well, under the current state of the law, not only am I free from all liability of the actions of the fraudulent handymen, but I can continue allowing the handymen to advertise on my site to find more victims after I'm told that they're stealing.

The service providers technically do not write the content, so the words are free speech and the providers are immune.

This is a massive inefficiency and injustice in our modern commercial world. Nowhere else is one part of the ecosystem allowed to facilitate fraud, reap profits from doing so, and be legally protected by federal statute from any of the damage caused by that fraud. But that's where we are in the summer of 2015.

According to a source that wishes to remain unnamed:

"I worked with this guy in [REDACTED], and for just his fake businesses he would spend $100,000 a month on AdWords advertising because it made him so much money. That's why all these fake ads keep coming up, they advertise $15 service, but charge $200 or more and that covers the cost of advertising on Google plus tons of profit."

As of filing of the suit, there were 150 licensed locksmiths in the state of Maryland. Yet, there was more than double that number of locksmiths advertising services in Maryland. You don't have to be Steven Hawking to do that math. The search engines are perpetuating fraud. And they won't stop until we make them.

OTHER INVESTIGATIONS

Let's say that you've been scammed by a locksmith. You call the police, report the name of the company, report the phone number, and they try and follow up on the lead. Well, they're not going to do a sting operation because you lost $300.[41] It's not grand theft. It's not a big deal to them. No one got hurt.

You're frustrated, so they tell you to file a complaint. This is exactly like the "report a problem" tool being broken. It's like giving a disconnected customer service number out to disgruntled customers. The police simply do not have the resources or the will to

---

[41]Though stinging them one at a time would make for a terrific reality show. I await your call, Hollywood.

investigate. They've got murders to solve. They're not going to go after these guys. They just aren't. So, they tell you to tell someone else. Building a comprehensive case against these scammers would require federal coordination, and even the FBI doesn't seem to know what to do with this.

Just like with the accuracy of the data itself, everybody wants to pass the buck. Being robbed of $300 is a violation of state law. Being robbed of $300 because someone used mail fraud is potentially a federal crime. And knowingly advertising a bait-and-switch scam that causes the $300 robbery...well that's apparently not illegal at all, as long as it's on the Internet and not anywhere else.

It's too complex of a problem for one agency to handle, and there's no one really spearheading this. If someone knows someone like Elizabeth Warren, she seems to be the type of person who would get involved and spearhead the different agencies to work together. She is probably the only politician that I can think of who stands up for the consumers first and takes things public for the good of the people. That is her mission and fight. I am sure there are many other politicians on both sides of the aisle who truly fight for consumers and their voting public, but she seems to be far and away the most determined. I will be sending her office a copy of this book in hopes that she reads it or at least uses it as a coaster. I know she is busy, but this is important, and to millions of business owners, absolutely vital to their way of life.

I also think that Bob Ferguson, Washington State's attorney general, may be able to get excited about this. The states can't rewrite federal law, but they can devote local resources to rooting out the individual scammers. They can also apply pressure to the federal government and lobby for change at the federal level.

Until someone coordinates systematic change, the victims will keep piling up. Someone sued the search engines in federal court. It made news everywhere. Nothing happened. I wiretapped the Secret Service and the FBI to draw attention to the issue. I made some well-armed friends and Google shut down Google Maps for six weeks. Then it was back to business as usual. The buck keeps getting passed, until it lands in the search providers' pocket.

Another Way to Go After the Scammers

The U.S. Postal Service is one of the third party tools that is used by the scammers to verify these fake businesses. We talked about how scammers use virtual credit cards to avoid detection, but that is not the only way that they do it. They don't even have to use fake cards when abusing the post office's system.

If you have online banking, which nearly everyone does, you can change your billing address on your debit or credit card online anytime you want. If you want to forward the mail for a company that does not exist, then no one will know if the mail goes missing. Therefore the post office will never get a notification that something is wrong, because no one had their mail stolen. Allow me to explain this in more detail.

Let's say that I change my billing address for my credit card at Bank of America from my home address to the address of a friend of mine for a prank. I put in a change of address, and it matches the address and zip code, and allows me to forward his mail. Now, when his mail stops showing up, he will complain, and ultimately, I will get caught in the subsequent investigation. I will go to jail. I will get more tattoos.

Now assume that I forward the mail of someone *who doesn't exist*. That person will never call anyone to complain that they did not receive their mail, because that person is a figment of my imagination.[42]

Substitute that imaginary person for an imaginary business. The business does not exist, yet you put in a change of address for it. So when mail arrives for that fake business to the original target address, it gets forwarded by the post office, no questions asked. They assume that if you somehow figured out how to forward someone else's mail, you would ultimately get caught and therefore avoid that fraudulent activity for fear of prosecution.

Imaginary companies and people can't call to report a problem, so these criminal scammers don't even need to go to extreme lengths

---

[42] Like my prom date. Just kidding, Jennifer Lawrence.

to abuse the postal service's website in order to accomplish their goals.

Hopefully the USPS will take a look at the abuse of its system and implement solutions that can detect this kind of activity. Here are some suggestions. Monitor change of address requests by IP Address and maintain a database of known VPN and other IP Address changing services to detect those who are trying to use the website change of address portal from behind VPN or other services that are used by criminals to hide their true identity.

They could also monitor names and card numbers to ensure that the same card number cannot be used over and over again, while changing the billing address to match the address verification form. This would force the scammers to get multiple credit cards, which would be a financial burden that would deter some of the lower level types.

They could monitor business names, and potentially flag certain keywords for manual review. Carpet cleaners, garage door repair, and locksmiths would be my first three choices.

As I have mentioned before, there could be a sharing of information agreement of some kind where the Postal Service could connect with local and federal databases of companies so that they may check to see if the business is even legitimate. Hell, I am sure the IRS would love to know about all these so-called business-forwarding requests so that they could formally introduce themselves.

I know that the IRS would love to investigate massive fraud, and this way multiple government agencies could share expenses and resources to ensure that people are playing by the rules.

After the Postal Service, all we're left with is the IRS. Though you might think it hard to imagine a less sympathetic institution than the IRS, it is arguably the single biggest victim of cyber fraud.

According to Dan Austin and Mark Baldino, in not just the locksmith industry but all of the other industries combined, the figure that is leaving the United States and not being taxed is between 10 and 20 billion dollars per year. Mark estimates in just the locksmith business alone, it's a billion dollars a year that is pulled out of our economy. If it were taxed at even 20%, that billions of dollars per year that is not being spent on bridges, highways, and death panels.

Ali, one of the locksmiths in [REDACTED], talked about before the Internet age, there was a man he grew up with who became a locksmith scammer, while he went the legitimate route. Ali ran a legitimate business while this guy was making 10 to 20 million dollars a year for 10-plus years. Ali is still working hard; his childhood friend now travels the world on a yacht with his wife and children. He built fake businesses in the Yellow Pages and 411 directories all over the United States, Canada and Europe. His organization got to the point where it made so much money that the men behind it eventually just retired and left the country. He's not even in the United States. If we wanted to prosecute him, there really is nothing we could do. You'd have to find him on his yacht.

These are the kinds of people that we're dealing with. The really big fish scam as hard as they can on a broad scale, and then walk away with bags filled to the brim with cash. All of it tax-free.

Summary

As you can see, this is not a one-man crusade against Internet service providers. There are thousands of documented victims from around the country, locksmiths suing the ISP's in federal court, investigations from Attorneys General, as well as numerous blogs and journalists calling attention to the issue. The ISP's got the case dismissed, which took the wind out of the sails of many people across the country.

There were so many people counting on Google in particular, due to its size and influence, finally being forced to do the right thing. Why is doing the right thing so hard? Because it means losing a lot of money. The directories are telling us loud and clear that they prefer the money over doing the right thing. And a bizarre federal law insulates them completely from any liability for facilitating fraud; even fraud they know is being perpetrated through their sites.

The only way they are going to change is if we either force a change in the laws, or "vote with our keyboards" by boycotting the services that are exacerbating these problems. In the following chapters, I am going to show you just how you can help right these wrongs. We don't need to reinvent the wheel; we have the Internet. Every person reading this book can help put a stop to this, and every person reading this book matters. The business owners and consumers who have been voiceless and ignored are counting on you and me.

Here is an email I received when Mark Baldino's case was dismissed from one of the most knowledgeable sources on Google Maps Spam.

Bryan,
Mark's case was dismissed:
http://www.courthousenews.com/2015/01/30/search-engines-dodge-angry-locksmith-claims.htm
Your book is the only thing that stands between us and Lockageddon.

Okay, slight exaggeration, but I'm not really kidding. I think there's two part-time guys whose hobby it is to pull down locksmith spam via MM [Google Mapmaker] (not me), and a Google Reviewer who is still pretty active in responding to spam locksmith reports via Map Maker, but that's about it.

There's an ocean of untouchable spam that not even Google likes to respond to anymore, unless their spam filter catches it. My guess is they're still embarrassed (if the Goog Collective even feel such a thing) by the fact that they're going to have to play whack-a-mole with human reviewers forever, and they don't like that thought. Not one bit.

Skynet is disappointed that clever human spammers just won't give up and die. Skynet is not winning the war on spam.

Eight

Profile of a Handsome Hypothetical Scammer

Instead of giving you a lot of "general" information and talking about the who, what, when and why, I figured it would be more helpful to take you through the profile of a scamming company that is very much in business at this very moment.

Funny story: I very much wanted to use the company's actual name and the names of the people who worked there. Like, I actually wrote a whole draft with none of the names changed to protect the NOT innocent. I really thought I hit it out of the park. Then my lawyer got his hands on it.

After he regained consciousness and changed his underwear, he informed me that we would be going another direction. As in, the opposite direction, as fast as possible.

So now the names HAVE been changed, to protect me. In fact, as much as I love accuracy, let's just go ahead and say that, until further notice, this book is now fan fiction. I'm now just going to make up a story about a spamming company.

Once upon a time, there was a company called Monkeys Monkeys Monkeys Media, run by a woman named Sally "The Ape" Salamander (the nickname is ironic). Sally ran her empire out of a magical land called Cauliflorida. "4M", as we'll call it, had a very vague website, and tried to look just like any other website development, advertising and web services company.

4M pretended to make money by, let's say, selling frisbees. One day, a handsome if dopey man in need of work named "Adonis" stumbled into 4M. He needed money. 4M had money. You can see the mutual appeal. He was offered a job in "data entry".

Adonis quickly realized that this was not merely data entry. Instead, Adonis was an integral part of creating over 3,000 unique fake locations in cities all across the country. He even hired professional writers to author between 10,000 and 20,000 fake testimonials, which were then posted all over the Internet.

Unless you were on the inside, it would be extremely difficult to find these businesses, fake reviews, and websites and tie them all together. The scale of this operation got quite complex, and there were many challenges associated with running an operation of this size.

Planning

Where to build listings?

4M wanted to build 3,000 listings. But did it need to use 3,000 different cities? No, boys and girls, it did not.

Let's look at this from a population based planning model.

*Figure 9.1*xxviii

The areas in red are huge population centers. So you can add listings in those areas multiple times, as long as you have a good spacing between them. Think franchises. Big cities have more than one McDonald's, so why not other types of businesses?

According to data from the U.S. Census, there are nearly 300 cities with populations of 100,000 people or more.

If you were to look at the census information and broke down the data, you would be able to estimate that with 3 listings per 100,000 people, you would conservatively get 2,319 listings.

City Sizes	# of Cities	# of Listings
100k-200k	185	555
200k-300k	45	270
300k-400k	28	252
400k-500k	10	120
500k-600k	7	105
600k-700k	8	144
700k-800k	4	84
800k-900k	3	72
900k-1 Million	1	27
1.1 Million	1	33
1.3 Million	2	78
1.4 Million	1	42
1.5 Million	1	45
2.0 Million	1	60
2.6 Million	1	78
3.7 Million	1	111
8.1 Million	1	243

Figure 9.2

There could easily be different brand names, and you would be able to dominate every spot in the search results. What would happen if you were results 1, 2, 3, 4, 5, and 6? You would get every single call, and then sell them to the real companies at a mark up.

It sounds ridiculous, doesn't it? Like sweet, sweet fiction for which nobody could be sued.

Check out this screen shot:

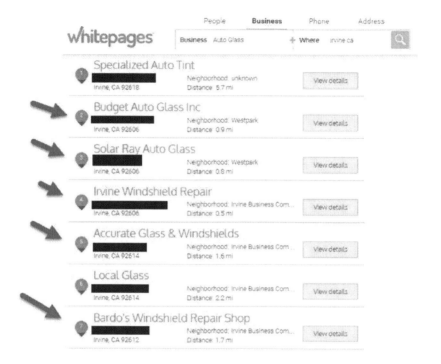

Figure 9.3

See the results? If you look these up, you are going to see Blue results before the orange ones. Those are paid advertising, not "organic" results. Organic results are the ones that are free and not promoted by the business. I would generally say that this makes them more reliable. In this case, that is 100% the opposite.

The names with red arrows are all controlled by the same scammer organization. They all have phone numbers that are provided by one specific site for bogus telephone numbers.

All of these businesses are like Freddie Krueger from "A Nightmare on Elm Street". They only exist in your mind, and they hurt you. They have no business license. There is no store, no guy with a van, no warehouse with parts and glass neatly stacked.

They only exist on these mapping directories. The directories are providing you, like all of the other sites, information that you want. They want information from businesses so that they will have information to show you, the consumer. So business owners get more business by sending their information to the search engines, and the search engines get more consumers who want that information. It seems like a perfect solution. Unless all the results are made up.

And who is the mastermind behind all of this? Sally, and all of Sally's minions, like Adonis. Sally was laughing all the way to the bank. And not only that, but she can go to the bank any time of day because she doesn't have to have a normal job. Her 1.2 million dollar home in Cauliflorida is less than a minute from the bank, which she can walk to if she so chooses.

How to name fake business listings

When you try to build 3000 listings without having the same name, things start to get kind of tricky. 4M created "franchise" groups of 30-50 businesses that had the same naming scheme.

A combination of those variations, plus a simple surname, was very common.

Words like Budget, Thrifty, Cheap, Speedy, Rapid, Professional and other adjectives make a lot of possible combinations when you start running out of ideas for what to name a new company. But, as my exasperated attorney reminds me, those words can also be used to form legitimate companies. So please don't sue me, AAA Budget Thrifty Rapid Professional Enemas, Inc.!

How to find addresses for fake listings

When 4M was trying to plan for a new location for its fake businesses, the first approach was to just look at the map and find an address near the center of the city. Once it realized that this was extremely time consuming, 4M came up with a better way.

Think about what you are trying to find. Addresses where you can register a fictitious business without drawing any attention. They're out there. The answer may be obvious, if you've been paying attention to earlier chapters. It is...the private postal box stores. Since the business model caters to the local community, these stores are perfect for this purpose. All you have to do is search for a postal box store in the city you are trying to build in, and you will find a location that is safe to build a business listing.

Now these stores can be expensive. If you are going to be getting 3000+ locations, the cost is prohibitive, especially considering that it is a monthly charge for the service.

But what is the reason that you want the address? Is it so that you can receive correspondence for your business on a daily basis? No; it is so that you can get just one piece of correspondence from the search company (let's say that in our world, the biggest such company is called "Gaggle") that allows you to register your address and get your highly sought after maps listing. So you can run thousands of fake listings through one P.O. Box in a given locality.

Phone Numbers

4M needed phone numbers. Lots of phone numbers. There are a number of things that you have to consider when finding the right phone number provider. The basic features that 4M looked for were the ability to track and accurately generate reports for the calls, which would allow 4M to bill its clients and gauge other metrics. One of the most important things is cost. (A penny saved is a penny stolen.) With 3000+ locations, keeping the cost per number down is especially important.

There are plenty of companies that provide these services. They have words like "call" and "phone" and "ring" in them. But please don't sue me, Call Phone Ring Jewelry, Inc.!

Within the control panel that you get when you sign up, you would be able to purchase new phone numbers for your "marketing campaigns." These can be toll free numbers like 1800 or 888, as well as local numbers that give this company the ability to appear local when in reality they are not.

Once you have a destination, you can turn on call recording, notification for call recording (which tells the caller that the call might be monitored for quality assurance purposes) and a variety of routing and reporting options.

Once the calls routings are set up, you can run reports that aid in the ability to invoice clients, view growth in call volume and figure out where you need to boost call volume and which listings are doing poorly.

Domain Names

Domain name ordering is not something that all the main scammers do, but it is fairly common. To look like a legitimate business, you must attempt to do all the things that typical businesses do. It's 2015, and nearly every business out there has a website. Scammers are no exception. 4M also figured out that it needed to beat the typical business at SEO (Search Engine Optimization) and profile optimization so that it would rank higher than the other businesses.

In order to maximize the rank of their listings, 4M would purchase domain names that were very keyword saturated, which often ended up looking kind of ridiculous.

There used to be a list of these names. Then my lawyer saw it and gouged out one of his eyes. So now you'll just have to imagine what I'm talking about. Also, try to imagine my lawyer with an eye patch.

Setting Up New Email Accounts

When 4M went from just a few fake listings to a large-scale enterprise, it started measuring and calculating the amount of time that things require in order to reduce the amount of time it takes to build listings.

In order to build "Gaggle Places" listings, it needed Gaggle accounts that would allow you to create the listing. Well, you can't use the same one over and over, as Gaggle (a diligent and wise company) would get suspicious. So, 4M started creating them one by one by one. This was a huge gigantic pain in its fraudulent butt.

So 4M used Gaggle to search for bulk gagmail accounts, and sure enough, there were people who sold them in bulk. How they create them is basically the same way that you and I would, which is manually, except that they paid people in Bangladesh and other countries to do the work, at a much lower cost per hour. Think $1 an hour or less.

A batch of 100 gagmail accounts ran anywhere from $5-15 depending if they were created using a U.S. IP Address, phone verified or included the password recovery and reset options. There were a lot of options when purchasing them.

Note, this is how email spammers and other people get their accounts created. It makes more sense to pay a small fee than waste the time to create new emails over and over.

Here is what a file might have looked like after you received your purchased gagmail accounts:

E-Mail	Password
altha.spertzell@gagmail.com	6L4yL9RN
ligia.westerfeld@gagmail.com	2F5els6r
dorian.ifft@gagmail.com	idU0T35O
libbie.pfraum@gagmail.com	N791rqwW
tania.glueck@gagmail.com	X351GNlp
georgina.heyer@gagmail.com	146YSCpN
candelaria.kraft@gagmail.com	d1x84yBR
era.berges@gagmail.com	CPM93I7w
dakota.karsten7@gagmail.com	PAYz33x8
cassi.neidel@gagmail.com	B2ZA58Zg
hildred.moody@gagmail.com	61SKJI0L
peter.rough4@gagmail.com	508IBWjU
sherill.scheidemandel@gagmail.com	YB7G7UF5
kristan.vonsensburg@gagmail.com	K098KFjH

Figure 9.4

As you can see, they are organized, alphabetized, and include the relevant information that you need. Sometimes they would even have the recovery question and answer so that if you get locked out of the account, you can still recover the password.

Changing IP Address

Changing your IP address is another requirement that 4M had to do if it wanted its listings to stay online and generating phone calls. The IP address is what Gaggle would track when it made updates, and if it saw too many submissions from one address, it would absolutely ban the listing and the gagmail account used. You just paid good money for the gagmails, so why not be careful and use a different IP address? And so 4M did.

How They Changed It

4M could purchase a VPN account from a service provider online. There are many out there. VPN services typically provide you with a piece of software that connects to their system and makes it very easy to connect to different servers from your laptop or computer at home. The websites you visit while connected to these services make it appear as if you are connected from a different location than you really are, which gives you some additional privacy and in this case, hides the fact that you are really one person instead of the hundreds of people you are pretending to be.

You can order proxy IP addresses. The advantage is that you can order a proxy IP address for a listing, and keep that IP address for the individual business listing that you assign it to. This allowed 4M to maintain a consistent IP address for each Gaggle listing it set up and made it very hard for Gaggle or other sites to detect its real identity.

If you have a cell phone from Verizon, AT&T or other major provider, you can also use "tethering," which is using your phone as a mobile hotspot. If you use the tethering feature, and want to change your IP address, you can just turn on Airplane Mode or reset the phone, which gives you a brand new IP address every time your phone connects to the network.

Clearing Cookies

Depending on which browser you are using, clearing cookies was also very important when working on listings. A HTTP cookie (also called web cookie, Internet cookie, browser cookie or simply cookie[43]), is a small piece of data sent from a website and stored in a user's web browser while the user is browsing that website. Every time the user loads the website, the browser sends the cookie back to the server to notify the website of the user's previous activity.[xxix]

There are browser plug-ins and applications that are very easy to use and install. The penalty for not doing this every time is getting your listings flagged or banned, and therefore no phone calls and no money.

---

[43]Nom nom nom.

Hiring Help

One thing that 4M figured out when growing its operation was that good help was hard to find. Paying people in the United States was expensive, and finding people who were consistent and reliable became a big challenge.

4M found that hiring people in the Philippines was a good alternative to paying workers here. By posting a simple ad on Craigslist in Manila, Adonis found some very good employees – as many as 8 at a time - to work 40+ hours a week on various tasks. The best part was that they pay ranged from $2-4 an hour. Which is both highly shameful and among the least shameful aspects of this enterprise.

Reviews Fraud

4M realized very quickly that the call volume that their fake listings received was very much affected by the ranking on Gaggle Maps. They didn't build their listings exclusively on Gaggle Maps, but dozens of others sites at a minimum. Adonis learned quickly that Gaggle was by far the most important site in terms of driving call volume.

One of the main ranking factors was review quality and quantity. So 4M decided to simply fake the 5 star reviews that they needed. Given that the listings themselves were fake, faking reviews was just more of the same thing. You have the time, you have the tools, and thanks to the Philippines, you have the low-cost labor. Now we just had to figure out how to actually accomplish this.

How are you going to write thousands of fake reviews? 4M found out very early that duplicate reviews get flagged and the listings removed because the reviews were the same. Gaggle had duplicate content checking thresholds that would catch the lazy spammer. (Again, Gaggle is a very diligent, wise, and handsome company.)

When 4M was at about 300 listings, we paid someone to post reviews. But we were not specific or thorough enough in our instructions, and he ended up making a simple mistake that cost everyone a lot of time and money.

He used the same email account to post the same review (word for word) from the same IP address on numerous listings.

Nearly overnight, all the listings were removed by Gaggle's fraud detection tools. Yes, Gaggle had tools in place to detect really lazy and careless spam. So that taught them a valuable lesson.

When those listings came down, call volume disappeared instantly.

4M could have just given up, called it a day, and pursued legitimate employment. Instead, they did the honorable thing and hired several underemployed professional writers. One of them was a screenwriter who needed a job to feed his family and pay his bills. He had previously written wonderful movies and television shows. But we paid him quite a lot to write unique, customized, keyword targeted reviews. He wrote a lot of them. He is now a big shot in Hollywood.

Here are some completely made-up examples of the type of reviews that he wrote:

Easter Sunday. the family dressed happy on our way to church. We're on the freeway a work truck tarp loosened and gravel started jumping on my windshield and the body of my car. The windshield had dozens of chips and needed replacement. Well I did my best to keep my spirits up. After the service I call a local great 24/7 glass replacement shop who gave me an appointment the next morning. God Bless the great glass replacement Shop.

Thanks for the incredible auto glass repair. I truly could not believe how quickly the job was done, and the new window looks great! Thanks again!

My insurance company recommended this company. Being helpful they actually called to make an appointment for my windshield repairs. The glass replacement tech came out in the rain and replaced the windshield under a carport and did an excellent job. I would highly recommend them to anyone.

"Affordable Auto Glass! I was at my dealership and they gave me an outrageous price. I called this wonderful glass replacement shop and it was over 80% off what the dealer quoted me to replace my windshield! They were quick and helpful. I drove off with a beautiful piece of work. I would recommend anyone to come ...

I have been a customer for 15 years at this auto glass place. They have been providing me with a great service, fast installation, and very affordable price. If you want your car to be effortlessly taken care of this is your glass shop.

This is my second time coming to the best affordable glass shop in town this past month with two different vehicles. Both times they have done a fantastic job and the customer service is amazing. I could not afford repairs at the dealership. The owner, a good guy, gave me a discount enabling me to take care of my cars. Thanks for your help.

Fast and efficient..I arrived at 8:15 and was out the door at 9:00. I have a 2009 A.4 Audi TSX with a "spider web" crack. Their price VERY reasonable and beat all of the other estimates I had. GREAT WORK! GREAT PRICE!

Awesome! Today I visited this glass repair garage place. I had a very noticeable chip on my windshield. For a very reasonable price they repaired it. Now I can not even see the chip! I waited a little less than an hour. The repair turned out much better than I expected. The tech guys are just awesome. Thank you so much.

GREAT JOB! LOVE IT . THEY WERE FAST AND EASY TO LOCATE.

In all, he wrote over 10,000 custom reviews. It sounds ridiculous, I know. And yet it's true. I mean, it's fan fiction.

The best part was that even though we couldn't use them more than once on Gaggle Maps, we could recycle them on other sites. The various sites collected reviews about companies from other sources and displayed them, which worked to 4M's advantage.

And if you wish really hard, say "Monkeys" four times fast, and enter any of the reviews above into a search engine, they say that numerous of these reviews will magically appear in your search results. Feel free to try it…but only if you believe in magic.

And if you don't believe in magic, as a shortcut I created some very simple links for you to type in that will allow you see the search results for yourself.

1. http://bit.ly/FakeReview-1
2. http://bit.ly/FakeReview-2

Figure 9.5

Quick Note

Your results might look different because I use a plug-in on my browser that disables advertisements. It disables ads on searches on many other sites. In addition to making the web a much more pleasant experience, it also saves a lot in loading times for browsers, which is handy when you have slow Internet speeds. https://adblockplus.org/ If you like the software, use it; it's free. You can donate money to the author, which I encourage. Also, in case you were wondering, I don't work for them and will not get any "commission" at all. I am a big advocate of open source software and if more of us supported guys like this, the Internet would be a better place.

Believe it or not, 4M made every single one of these business listings. The reviews were written in bulk and posted on many different sites to get the maximum amount of usage out of the reviews. The reviews were not cheap, and if you couldn't use them on Gaggle more than once, you might as well get your mileage out of each one.

As long as they were not posted to Gaggle listings directly more than once, no one would ever notice.

When you have an organization like this that sees the tangible, measurable and monetary value in various strategies, this type of thing is an absolute necessity. The rankings of the listings go up when there are more reviews. The higher the ranking, the more people see the business listing. The more people who see it, the more people will call. More calls means bigger paychecks. Hypothetically.

Selling & Billing

Since this organization does not actually know how to repair glass, 4M had to find someone to service those calls. When the consumers called, we needed a legitimate service provider to accept the calls forwarded from our telephone number; the one that they called.

4M simply entered into business relationships with a handful of companies in each geographic area where the fake listings were listed in each area. Then they sold those companies the leads.

4M would look for a small business owner with several employees. Then Sally or her sales staff would call and set a meeting with the owner to negotiate a deal where the owner would service the calls that they were going to send his way.

Sally didn't reveal that the phone calls were coming from fake business listings, but simply said things like:

> "We are a media and advertising company that specializes in Lead Generation."

or

> "We sometimes have 'overflow' or surplus calls all over the country and wanted to see if you would be interested in receiving them and paying a small fee for each."

This is not abnormal, as there are many different companies that specialize in nationwide lead generation and selling calls. Companies are more than happy to pay for leads in a variety of forms.

Web Leads

This is data that customers enter into websites requesting information.

Warm Phone Transfers

Phone calls that are transferred with an interested consumer on the line.

Hot Transfer

Consumer on the phone looking for a quote or purchase right then. This is the most valuable, and this is the type of lead that Sally sold.

The business owners typically responded well to this approach because for them, it was very simple mathematics.

Let's say that for every call they receive it costs them $10.00.

They make a sale on these calls 8 / 10 times.

The profit on each call is an average of $50, with a wide range depending on the service.

10 calls would cost them $100.00. 10 calls would generate $400.00 profit after costs (since only 8 generated revenue).

That is very easy for a business owner to agree to. Sally sets up the phone routing to route calls to the owners, and at the end of the month she sends them a bill for the calls.

This is an ~~actual~~ pretend bill from the sales of calls to an auto glass company:

Media/ **shields.com**		**INVOICE**			
			DATE:		8/22/2011
			INVOICE #		8222011AAGHTX
			Customer ID		Auto Glass | Houston TX
Ladera Ranch CA 92694			Due:		Upon receipt
Phone:					
Attn:					

BILL TO:

Auto Glass | Houston TX

DESCRIPTION

Unique Live Call Phone Leads for Auto Glass Service

Date Delivered	Unique Calls	Cost/Unique Call	Total
08/15/2011 - 08/21/2011	107	$8.00	$856.00

Notes: This Invoice does not include "Lost Prospect" or "No Answer Calls" as billable calls.

Figure 9.6

But what happens when the calls are from telemarketers or wrong number? Does the customer get charged for every call? No. This happens a lot.

What happened was that all the calls were sorted, filtered for duplicates, and only calls that were longer than 60 seconds were invoiced. Typically if it was a wrong number or someone selling the shop something, the customer representative got rid of them in less than a minute and they were not charged.

Now if the business owner wanted to dispute things, which happened frequently, Sally had all the calls set to be recorded, and could play back any disputed calls. This was a really simple way of figuring out if the caller was a lead or not.

Though some would grouse here and there, ultimately the business owners paid for the calls so they would keep coming. Every once in a while, Sally and her sales staff would have to find someone else to receive those calls. It was never difficult.

Remember though, if there were no fake listings, the consumers would be calling these companies directly, without this added middleman. In many places, the fake listings setup by Sally dominated most of the top spots which consumers call first. Consumers are calling the top rated companies but being connected to the ones on page 2 and 3.

How rampant is this problem? Well, let's speculate. It's all just make-believe anyway, remember? Take a look at these totally-fictitious call reports for August 2011. One of the last months Adonis was involved with 4M. They had a total of 18,600 calls in the month of August. You can see some of the "campaigns", Albuquerque, Philadelphia, Jacksonville, and the list goes on. Obviously the ones with the higher numbers of leads are bigger cities since they have more potential consumers. It is also harder to rank in those cities.

18,600 calls spread over 31 days in August is weirdly 600 exactly. 4M was not in every state. There were many cities where they did not have clients purchasing calls, so they had not set up listings there yet. Even in New York City, there were only two fake business locations. The states with the most fake listings were California, Ohio, Illinois, Michigan, Washington, Arizona, and Texas.

Six hundred calls every single day. That's just one scamming organization, in only one industry. There are so many other industries where this type of scamming is present it barely scratches the surface of just how bad this problem is.

600 calls per day, with the average price of a listing being $8.00 each. $4800 per day, $1,747,200 per year.

Some of the calls might be discounted or priced higher depending on the client, but this gives you an idea of what this organization made based on one month in 2011. In all likelihood they would have grown, adapted and could very well be doing much more volume. None of this income is taxed.

Wasn't that a frightening story, boys and girls? It certainly terrified my lawyer.

There will always be people trying to find ways to gain a competitive edge, whether it is an athlete taking steroids, a jockey losing weight to win the Kentucky Derby, or a business owner trying to find a way to live the American Dream. There is a difference between trying to live the American dream, and robbing thousands of their ability to do so.

Scammers like this hide in the shadows and many of them will stop at nothing in their pursuit of money. They don't care that they are putting people out of work with their tactics, which ultimately hurts consumers and the overall economy in the entire country. With your help, this story can be transformed from fan fiction to ancient history.

Nine

How to Fight Back

"Be the change you wish to see in the world." -Two dimes

Chapter 6 listed several solutions to the maps fraud problem. However, unless you happen to run a multi-billion dollar search engine, you are likely powerless to implement those solutions.

The good news is that this book also contains solutions that we can implement in our daily lives and share with the people we know. While the crooks are undoubtedly facilitated in their crimes by the poorly written laws regulating the search engines and their lack of internal standards, ultimately every one of these crimes requires an unwitting consumer victim. The purpose of this chapter is to make you more witting.

I know that there are many others who share my view on this, which is why I was asked to give a TEDx talk on April 11, 2015 on this very subject. Trying to pack this subject into a 300-page book was difficult. Packing it into an 18-minute talk was virtually impossible.

I didn't write this book for personal gain or because I wanted a place to vent my frustration. Yes, I am frustrated. It's a lot like watching a smaller kid get picked on by a bully and seeing teachers laughing at the younger one for being helpless.

Whether you are merely affected by maps fraud as a consumer or also impacted as a business owner, this chapter has advice to ensure that you are not enriching the scammers in any way whatsoever.

How to Spot Fake Listings

Much of this advice comes down to two simple tips: learn how to spot fake listings and avoid them. I'll walk you through the whole process, and by the end you should have a very good understanding of what spam experts look for when assessing the legitimacy of a business listing.

In this screen, you can see results A-H:

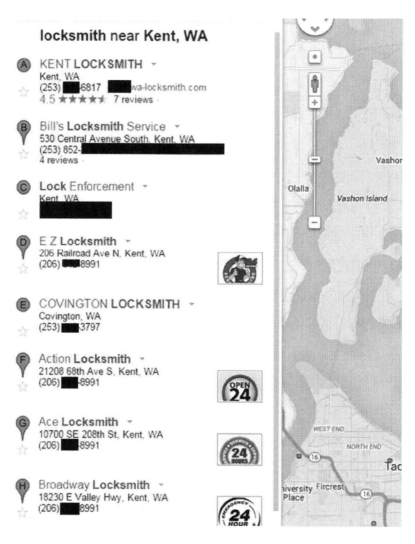

Figure 9.1 - It's funny how four of the listings in this screenshot have the exact same phone number.

There are a few components that are standard for map listings, which include:

Business Name
Address
Phone Number
Website
Reviews
Pictures

and the little (A) Figure 1.72 or (B) Figure 1.73.

The Circle means that the business listing creator doesn't want to show their address. The 'pin' means the business displays their address. This is what the search engines refer to as a "storefront" business. If a business won't display its address, it is referred to as a "Service-Area-Business".

Here are some tips you can use to determine if a business is fake based on first glance and it may help you select one that is legitimate.

Business Names:

When you are looking for a business in the "locksmith" category, the easiest way to recognize a likely fake[44] is when you see "CITYNAME + CATEGORY" such as:

---

[44] Note the word "likely". There is a chance that a real business could legitimately think that these naming conventions are real. Just like there is a chance that the beautiful woman you met on Facebook only won't talk to you on the phone because she only messages you from work and she'd get in trouble with her boss.

Results A, E. Kent Locksmith and Covington Locksmith seem likely offenders in this search. Most businesses don't name themselves something so generic. This is a red flag. I believe that Bill's Locksmith Service is an actual locksmith, because (among other reasons) it has a business license.

Pictures:

If you look at just the thumbnail picture first, you can usually tell if the photo is of the business, a logo, or something that looks like stock photography. If you look at F, G, and H, you will see that they have very similar graphics. This is something to watch for, as these are likely to be scammers. Here's a corollary tip for legitimate businesses: Don't use stock footage. And if you're a beautiful woman trolling Facebook for sensitive nerds, sneak away from your desk for a couple minutes and call them. It will greatly ease their skepticism.

Reviews:

Just looking at the number of reviews is not helpful unless you see that they are well into the double digits. Few scammers bother to make that many reviews for one fake business. Having double digit reviews means the business typically would have been online for some time and subject to a number of consumers viewing that business. When it has been online for years, chances are it is legitimate.

Such as result A, which is a likely scammer (7 reviews). Result B is Bill's Locksmith Service, and is likely a real licensed company.

If you want to know what fake reviews look like, then this is your lucky day. These are the reviews from XXXXX LOCKSMITH in result A.

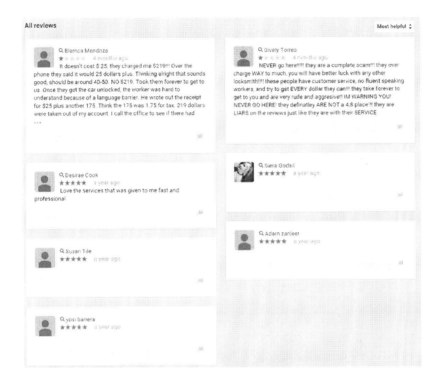

Figure 9.2

Five reviews that are 5-star all from a year ago. Only one of them actually has a written review. Two have very recent reviews that are one star. Don't you think it is a little strange that there are no 4 star or 3 star reviews?

Oh! The most important thing is that, 4 months ago, someone is describing how this business advertised $25 services and charged over $219.00 when they arrived. This is what I was talking about in regards to bait & switch advertising.

This business can't be reported to the Better Business Bureau or local government. From their perspective, this is nothing more than a lie posted on someone's property. The government will tell you to take it up with the search engine that publicized the lie. The search engine can hide behind existing law, and there is a 260-page book reduced to two sentences. The criminals are paying the search companies to allow them to advertise these fake prices for the fake businesses and the companies willingly accept the money.

When you are looking at reviews, you can click on the person who left the review:

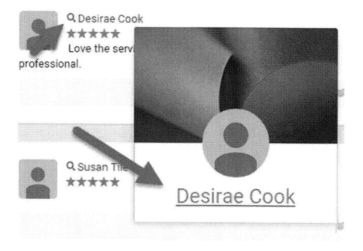

Figure 9.3

Then you will see that user's page. Then click on the Reviews

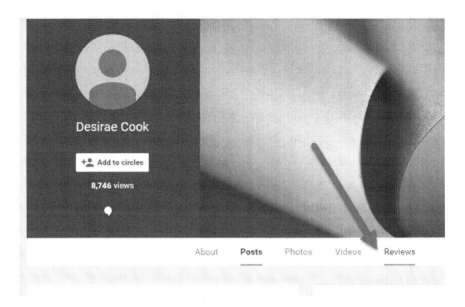

Figure 9.4

Now you are going to see all the reviews that that user has posted over the course of their time on this site. If a user has one review and it is from a locksmith, it is almost certainly a fake.

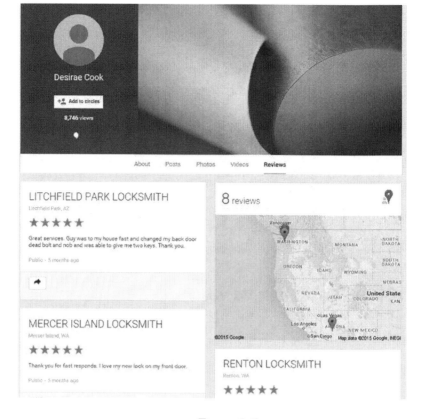

Figure 9.5

This user has reviewed seven locksmiths and towards the bottom, one garage door repair business. This is the second most spammed category in the business. The people behind this account are likely the ones behind the building of the fake listings and, as you can see here, this user reviewed eight of their businesses. The only other explanation is that this person loses their keys incredibly often.

You can do this research just as I did to find out if a business is shady or not. You can determine if there are fake reviews or not.

Would you want to go to a business that has misrepresented its services? I certainly wouldn't.

Websites:

It is generally more difficult to tell if a business is fake based on its website. Lots of people have figured out that it is a good idea to match the business name to the website name as closely as possible. This is good for SEO (Search Engine Optimization) but also can be helpful when identifying spammers. At least it's one more thing to watch for.

Result A: ██████wa-locksmith.com

This isn't much different, but it's still fishy enough. Once you go to the site, you can see that it is pretty generic with nothing that shows where they are or talks about who will be coming to your home. You want to find business license information, or photos of the business, or the technicians. You need to be certain you are calling a real business, not some guy out to scam you. Look for evidence that the business actually exists.

If you notice a naming pattern in websites within a similar category, chances are that you have found a scammer operation. The two websites below are likely part of the same organization. As you can see they use windshield repair or auto glass repair after the city or region name. These appear as though they were all bought and paid for at the same time, built at the same time, and the websites are nearly identical.

SAN JUAN CAPISTRANO Windshield Repair
"San Juan Cap's Choice For Rock Chip Repair"
(949) 467-1452

Figure 9.6

RANCHO SANTA MARGARITA Windshield Repair
"Rancho Santa Margarita's Choice For Rock Chip Repair"
(949) 467-1452

Figure 9.7

Wow, the phone numbers are even identical; they just changed the color slightly and switched the BMW for a Honda.

When it comes to a website, if the price seems too good to be true, or it seems really generic, that's a huge red flag. If your radar is telling you that this might be fake, then find a business that doesn't feel that way to you.

Address:

Remember the little circles and push pins? When a legitimate retail business is displayed online, it shouldn't feel the need to hide its address. Businesses that provide services don't necessarily have customers visit their locations, and many legitimate businesses could operate for decades without having a single customer at their office.

As I detailed earlier, you would never expect to visit your plumber, landscaper, carpet cleaner or other home service company at their office. They would be coming to you to clean, fix or install something at your home or business.

Google, for example, decided that they would implement "Service Area Business" as an option. When you check this box in the control panel for your business listing, it effectively hides a business address from consumers on Google Maps.

This is Google's description of what SAB's are.[xxx]

Service-area businesses on Google

Not all local businesses serve their customers from a brick-and-mortar storefront. For example, some businesses operate from a home address. Others are mobile and have no central location.

If your business serves customers at *their* locations, you should list it as a service area business on Google.

Add a service area

View full list

Step 1 of 4

Log in to Google My Business and choose the page you'd like to manage.

.//www.examp...

Manage this page

You will be able to set service areas based on the zip codes or cities you serve, or on a given area around your location.

You additionally have the option to indicate **I serve customers at my business address**. You should only select this option if you want your complete address to display on Google and if your business location is staffed and able to receive customers during its stated hours.

What's changed?

If you previously used the old Places for Business dashboard, you'll notice that we no longer have the **Do not show my business address on my Maps** option. We will apply the correct address settings for your business based on your choices from the new dashboard and the nature of your business.

Note: Some verified businesses will require another round of verification for changes in address.

Figure 9.8

Now, it's important to realize that there are some businesses that have hidden their addresses and are not scammers. However, virtually every scammer uses this feature. So if you already have an idea that the business looks a little shady, and you see instead of

then it's likely a fake business.

Again, a corollary tip: If you're a legitimate business, think very seriously about whether you need to hide your address. If you do, at least have a clearly searchable business license so that someone following these steps could conclude that you're not a fraud.

Why do some businesses hide their addresses? The two main reasons businesses hide their addresses are to avoid people actually visiting their office and because of a problem I addressed earlier with the "report a problem" link. To refresh your memory:

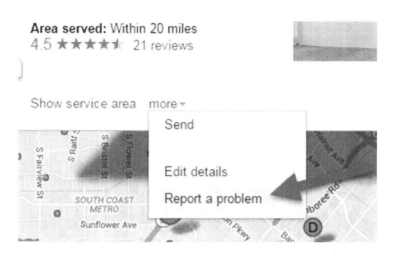

Figure 9.9

You can click on a business listing, and go to the "more", then "report a problem" link. But if the business is a Ⓐ instead of Ⓑ (meaning service area business), then the link does not work. You end up with this.

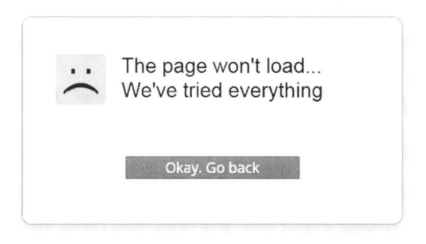

Figure 9.10

Technically, you don't have to do any of the above steps if you don't want to. What you can do to verify for sure is to go to your state's Business License search website, and search for the business you are trying to verify.

The search engines could easily find a way to cross-check these government databases, but as of now neither the law nor the marketplace compels them to do it. I would think that local government would gladly help aid the search engines in improving their verification techniques. It's exactly the kind of consumer protection work that attorneys general exist to adopt.

For the link to your state's business license search and much more visit:

www.cyberfraudtheweboflies.com/links

If you check your state's records and find that a business does not have a license, there are many things that you can do as a consumer, business owner, or concerned citizen that will make a real difference, and you will find all of that information towards the end of this chapter.

Leave Positive Reviews of Legitimate Businesses

This may seem like a small thing, but it isn't. A huge reason that the scammers can outperform real businesses is that people rarely take the time to leave a positive review for a legitimate business.

That means that the spammers can leave 5-7 fake reviews and be confident that they will outpace their honest counterparts.

You and I can help change our culture for the better. If you have a positive experience with a business, then the next time you're online, take 30 seconds to leave a positive review before you head over to Facebook or YouTube to while away your leisure time.

Leave a 3 or 4 star review if that's what was earned. If the real businesses got reviews from even 1% of their customers, much of the cyber fraud problem would disappear in days. Take it from someone who knows; legitimate looking fake reviews are expensive to generate in the bulk needed to move the needle for the scammers.

SEO Like a Pro

If you are a business owner, then you are going to want to highlight this section. I mean it: you could buy thousands of dollars in SEO services, books or videos and get virtually the exact same information here without having to pay an extra dime.

The reason I am giving you all of this information is to help you build your company's online presence better, which will give you a better chance of outranking the scammers. The scammers have a head start, but they can't possibly fight back against every single business in every city in America. If people share and help each other with honest reviews, feedback and advice, we can push these scammers' business listings out of the rankings and make the price they have to pay become so large that it is no longer cost effective to build fake listings. Part of the reason that it is working so well for scammers now is that most people aren't doing all of the things they need to do to be able to combat the criminals.

There are two parts of your business that we are going to talk about in this section: Your local business listings and your website.

Local Business Listings

Owning your own business can be a challenge. On top of the underlying industry in which you have to compete to survive, you also have to learn all sorts of computer skills just to get online so that consumers can find you. Fortunately, it is not as complicated as you might think, and I want to give you the most valuable information that I have learned so that you can worry about other things. Like zombies. Zombies are dangerous and wholly immune to these search engine optimization techniques.

The first thing you want to do is get your business information on as many major sites as possible. These websites are all directories, like the old telephone book, and help consumers find you. The more sites you are on, the more chances consumers have to find your business.

Here are some tips for your local business listing:

Make sure that your business name, address and phone number are consistent on all of the websites to which you submit.

Note: Websites like www.moz.com have a tool that checks other sites for consistency and helps you fix them.

Fill out every field you can. Most of these sites show you a percentage rating of your listing to let you know how "complete" your listing is. Follow their instructions to maximize the percentage. Most websites don't tell you how they calculate ranking, but they each have a system and it typically rewards those who put time into their business profiles.

Add as many relevant pictures as you are allowed.

Ask your regular customers to review your business honestly. If you are doing a great job, people should know about it.

Don't ignore social media. A Facebook page is a great start.

One thing I have noticed that has helped me a lot in the SEO space is that you should do some research in your city by category. If you are a restaurant in Chicago, go online and search for restaurants near your zip code.

Then look for the top ranked businesses and try to make yours look like theirs. Ask for reviews, but don't you dare write them yourself; however tempted you might be.

The important thing to realize is that you know the road map and the way to succeed in the online world. When you have no idea where to even start, most people won't even try. To help you along, here are a couple of really good services that provide great resources for business owners.

These companies will help you publish and spread your company's information to dozens of websites automatically, saving you a lot of time and energy learning.

- Moz.com – https://moz.com/local
- WhiteSpark.ca - http://www.whitespark.ca/

They have a variety of pricing models. Moz is a little bit cheaper, but the two services both have very high customer reviews. Like, real customer reviews.

Website

If you don't have a website, you need to get one. GoDaddy and many other sites offer simple hosting services, but I would recommend Dreamhost or GoDaddy for WordPress hosting. WordPress is a very simple website building tool that allows you to create custom website with zero programming knowledge. Most of the time you can just click and type in a few things.

Other options would be www.wix.com or any other website building services. There are so many out there now, and most of them have taken the guesswork out of the process.

If you want to learn more about local business marketing, here are a few websites that will help get you started.

- http://moz.com/blog
- http://searchengineland.com/
- http://blumenthals.com/blog/

If you need help getting started with a website, SEO, or just have questions, email me. Go to:

bryan@seelysecurity.com

I will be more than happy to answer questions and refer you to SEO specialists who can help you. I truly have that little to do. I'm not just being modest.[45]

Now What

I mentioned earlier that there are things that consumers and business owners can do in addition to the steps I have described. The first step is being able to recognize fake listings. Business owners can immediately help themselves by making their business listings better, but those can't be the only solutions for the general public. For those that have been scammed, here are some steps that you can take to ensure that it is properly reported.

File a complaint with the Federal Trade Commission (FTC)

http://www.consumer.ftc.gov/media/video-0054-how-file-complaint

File a complaint with your state Attorney General's office.

File a complaint with the Better Business Bureau

Let me know, and I will help get you the resources that you need. Depending on what happened, you might be able to talk to a local

---

[45]Yes I am just being modest, Jennifer Lawrence.

news station, legal authorities, or other organizations. The more stories I have, the better I can make my case for change.

The above steps will do a lot of good if you are a consumer reporting a fraud or scammer, but there are a few other things that the general public can do to make a real difference and get enough attention to this issue. In the next and final chapter, I will recap everything we have talked about, as well a couple solutions that I need your help with.

I can't do this on my own. I have been trying. I wiretapped the government, for crying out loud! I tried to generate enough buzz on my own, and however "ill-advised" that stunt might have been, I really thought that it would be enough to get everyone to look at the problem, and force the search companies to fix the problems that have plagued business owners for so long. The story got some headlines, made some people look, and even the Secret Service thought it was case closed.

So now I want to make sure that business owners and consumers know what is going on and hopefully be able to show just how bad it is, and ask for just a few minutes of your time. I promise, this can be solved.

Ten

Final Thoughts

"Never doubt that a small group of thoughtful, committed citizens can change the world; indeed, it's the only thing that ever has."
Margaret Mead

Throughout the last year, I have spent a lot of time telling people the information that I have laid out in this book. As time went on, I got better at explaining it in a shorter period of time. But I still can't do it in a few sentences.

The story is too complex to oversimplify and too important to try. Our shortening attention spans are exactly what the scammers feed on to steal business, and that same problem prevents people from learning how to make it stop.

It's important for me to convey the magnitude of the problem to you because up until now, it has not received the attention it deserves. Drawing attention to a problem that no one is paying attention to is very difficult to do by yourself. The fight needs to be legitimized, formalized, and brought to the public.

This problem needs attention because the victims of this systematic fraud and hostile online environment deserve help. Some of them have been victimized directly, others indirectly, but the results are bad, worse, or catastrophic. These are your friends, family, and neighbors. These problems are not isolated to one state. Such problems have fully spread to every city in the country. It is like a parasite. You typically don't notice how bad it is until your house is falling down, or when you inspect the wreckage.

What is the ideal result?

I have been asked this question a lot over the past year. Typically I try to keep it short, but I don't have to do that here. The victims are my main priority and the reason that I wrote this book in the first place.

The ideal solution would be eliminating these fake listings on the biggest websites so that all consumers – even the ones unwilling to undertake the basic steps to identify scammers -- would have a safer experience and business owners would get a fair shot. Business owners are being stolen from, consumers overcharged, and no one with the power to solve the problem is doing it.

Ideally, these companies would decide to clean up their own systems, put adequate controls in place, and work toward providing the cleanest and most accurate data they can. We know that they are not, and I have explained how in a number of ways throughout this book.

Failing that, the federal government could enact legislation that repeals the immunity search engines currently enjoy; at least for propagating knowingly false information. I'm not saying that the Googles of the world should have to write checks every time a customer gets baited and switched. But if a search engine knows that there's a given piece of fraud in their mall and they willfully choose not to remove it, then at least a jury should be able to decide if the "landlord" is liable. The case shouldn't simply be thrown out of court because the law protect the major companies at the expense of the little guy. Mark Baldino might not be entitled to millions, but his case shouldn't be thrown out of court without a chance to prove his claims.

Now I'm going to talk about Google for a minute[46]

Google is an amazing company, filled with extremely smart, dedicated, and ethical people. However, in my sole and un-actionable opinion, the leadership of the Google Maps portion of Google seems to be misrepresenting Google's mission to the world. Google Maps, its leadership, and the associated advertising part of its products, seem to be putting profitability over decency. That's how my lawyer told me to phrase it.

What I'm going to also write is that, in my opinion, maps fraud is a cancer. When a person gets cancer, it starts out as a small thing and quickly grows bigger and bigger until it is either cut out or the

---

[46]Really, Bryan? You are so close to getting out of this book without getting sued.

person dies. I don't know where things went wrong, but I am betting that it started when someone started lying, chasing money, or some combination of the two.

Maybe the revenue stream that would be lost would make someone look bad, or maybe someone had just bought a yacht and needed to pay it off. I know that the founders of Google have demonstrated that they are strong advocates of consumers, privacy, open-source software, and ultimately a commitment to bettering the world and the people in it.

So what the hell happened with the leadership at Maps, and how has it gone on for so long? Ultimately, I don't care how it happened. I just want it to stop. It's not too late.

I Need Your Help

I started this fight from my house. I was able to convince a reporter and camerawoman that things were bad. I kept telling the story. More news outlets, more people, and slowly the story developed. People all over have been fighting spam, but most of those people haven't made any real progress.

What I have learned is that I won't be able to solve this on my own, but that doesn't mean I won't try. My determination and passion for solving this problem resulted in being given a chance to tell a wider audience at a TEDx event, where the audience saw just a few PowerPoint slides and 15 minutes of summarizing what is in this book.

Some were shocked, many were confused (a few were aroused), and they could not stop asking questions. I hope that this is a good sign that this book will find its mark. Business owners don't deserve this, consumers don't deserve this, and I know that I am not alone in this fight.

Instead of continuing to hope that these companies decide to fix the problem, we are going to have to convince them that it is in their best interest to fix it. Many times, that is hitting them in the one area that they feel it the most....their wallets. So here is an action plan for you.

To Do List

Tell your friends about this book. Order it for a friend, colleague, or a business owner.

Add me on Linkedin.com and Twitter to find out more about how to help. Social media is an amazing way to get the word out about problems, and with your help, we can actually solve this.

Join my mailing list on seelysecurity.com and find out more updates as they happen.

To The Scammers

If you are one of the scammers that I am talking about, then this section is for you. I have a simple message: find a new line of work. The Internet has made the world a much smaller place, and I understand that it's tempting to make a quick buck. The Internet has also made it a lot easier to rally people to worthy causes, and this is absolutely a worthy cause. Loopholes open, get exploited, and close. With all due respect to "The Lion King", that is the economic circle of life.

This maps fraud loophole has been open for a long time. I get that. If a loophole exists long enough, it ceases to feel like a loophole and starts to feel like the way things ought to be. Well, it isn't. Our government has a history of protecting consumers from false commercial speech. It's been napping on the job when it comes to the Internet. But that era is winding to a close.

Sooner or later, they are going to get around to figuring out that the Internet should not be any different. And the first scammers working with impunity when that happens are going to prison. I believe it with every fiber of my being. I even hope to be called to testify as an expert witness.

I don't care if we have to hunt every single one of your fake listings down till the end of time and hire people at my own expense to do the job that the search engines are supposed to do. We are going to put a stop to this fraud.

That includes reporting you to every law enforcement agency in the country and making sure that every single business that operates without a license is reported to the state and to the IRS. You think that I am tenacious? Just wait until the IRS finds out that you aren't paying taxes. They don't give a crap if you are selling drugs illegally, but you damn sure better be paying your taxes on your profits or they are going to bring this fight to your doorstep faster than the men with badges and guns.

Bernie Madoff didn't think he would get caught, either. When a new crime emerges, there's always a first person to go to jail for it. But he got 150 years.

I know that some of you came to this country to abuse the system, but that time is coming to an end. If you don't have a legitimate business that plays by the rules, pack your bags and head home. Be the last one to get away with it instead of the first one to get caught.

The IRS, FBI and local Attorneys General are going to become aware of your existence and have a much easier time proving your guilt with all the evidence being served to them on a silver platter.

I am sending early copies of the book out immediately. One is going to my mom (love you, Mom!), and one to each of the 50 state Attorneys General. Another will go to the IRS, FBI and every major news network in the country. Many of them have already expressed interest in the story, and I know why. It's not every day that someone wiretaps the Secret Service to prove a point. The reason I didn't go to jail for it is because our government is smart enough to know that there are bigger fish to fry. Namely: you.

They didn't send me to prison, so you are going to have to tell me what it's like in there.

Let me know how the uniforms fit and how the food tastes. Tell me all about your new friends and your cozy room. And savor the irony of a fake locksmith getting locked behind the one lock they can't get through.

Epilogue

There have been a number of positive developments in the online maps world since the book was completed. As of May 2015, the problems that were detailed in these chapters, including screen shots, were all accurate. However, even during the pre-publication promotion of the book, I noticed that more and more of the loopholes I described were being closed, with new ones being opened again.

In addition to cosmetic changes, there have been some developments that have been very positive for consumers and small business owners. Some others, not so much.

The Android Peeing On Apple

As funny as this one was, I did not pull this prank. Kudos to the people who did. It was all over the Internet for a couple of days.

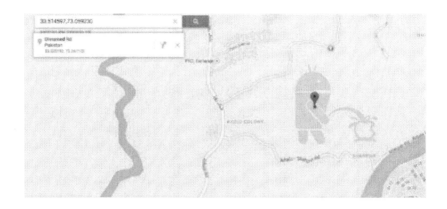

Google Maps Is Racist Now?

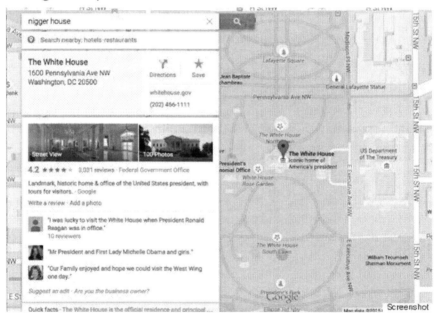

Screenshot

This next map-related blunder caused quite a stir in the online community. An individual on Twitter by the name Bomani X discovered that if you run a Google Maps search for the words "nigger house" or "nigger university", the results would show The

White House or Howard University, respectively. This story was in many major news outlets in a matter of hours. I was even called to appear on TMZ to speak with Harvey Levin and Charles Latibeaudiere about this truly shocking incident.

Google Mapmaker Shut Down Indefinitely

As of May 12, 2015, Google decided to suspend the Mapmaker product due to widespread problems. There were a variety of stories leading up to this final decision.

Give me some of the credit if you want to, but I neither need nor want it. What I want is for these developments to be the harbingers of major change, and not merely another blip on the radar screen. We can do it. And I truly believe that we will.

Acknowledgements

Cyber Fraud: The Web of Lies has been quite the undertaking, and would not have been possible without many people helping me along the way. Your support, advice and time spent helping me through this process means the world to me. In no particular order

Viveka Von Rosen, James Rosebush, Dayna Steele, Dan Austin, Mark Baldino, Dan Kawai, Yaz, Megan, Jerry, Heather, C. Long, Marty Reimer, Kareem, Robin, Shane Mauss and of course, my 3 wonderful children.

Thank you for the encouragement and support.

CREDITS

Proofreading & Editing

Lisa Seely

Jessica Whitehead

Cover Designer

Jonathan Chicquette

SOURCES

[i] https://en.wikipedia.org/wiki/419_scams

[ii] http://www.dailymail.co.uk/news/article-2974083/We-love-95-certain-s-telling-truth-Woman-defends-decision-wire-1-4-MILLION-online-lover-Africa-s-never-met.html

[iii] http://www.katu.com/news/local/34292654.html

[iv] http://www.nbcnews.com/id/8171053/ns/technology_and_science-security/t/nigerian-scams-keep-evolving/#.VQkoQY7F98E

[v] http://www.ksat.com/content/pns/ksat/news/2014/11/18/sa-man-arrested-in-nigerian-money-scam.html

[vi] https://cn.wikipedia.org/wiki/Bernard_Madoff

[vii] https://en.wikipedia.org/wiki/4-1-1

[viii] http://www.gpsbusinessnews.com/comScore-Google-Maps-App-

64-5M-Users-Apple-Maps-42M-in-the-U-S_a5012.html

ix http://www.dailymail.co.uk/sciencetech/article-2503432/Google-Maps-users-fall-THIRD-Apple-Maps-gain-ground.html

x https://www.schneier.com/blog/archives/2009/03/google_map_spa m.html

xi http://www.nbcnews.com/id/19714358/ns/business-consumer_news/t/locked-out-dont-fall-locksmith-scam/

xii http://www.theguardian.com/technology/2014/jul/08/restaurant-owner-sues-google-over-maps-listing-sabotage

xiii http://www.myfoxmemphis.com/story/27853749/mid-south-warned-of-locksmith-scam

xiv http://www.palmbeachdailynews.com/news/news/national/suspect-in-locksmith-scam-surrenders/nZbp3/

xv http://www.sacbee.com/news/business/personal-finance/claudia-buck/article3332607.html

xvi http://moz.com/learn/local/local-search-data-us

xvii https://moz.com/blog/2013-local-search-ecosystems

xviii https://www.ncta.com/platform/broadband-internet/how-google-tracks-traffic/

xix http://www.komonews.com/news/local/Google-Map-Jack-246585191.html

xx http://www.huffingtonpost.com/2013/09/23/fake-yelp-reviews_n_3976415.html

xxi http://www.komonews.com/news/local/Google-Map-Jack-246585191.html

xxii http://valleywag.gawker.com/how-a-hacker-intercepted-fbi-and-secret-service-calls-w-1531334747

xxiii http://gizmodo.com/its-ridiculously-easy-to-troll-google-maps-with-fake-l-1531646581

xxiv http://www.bloomberg.com/bw/articles/2014-03-28/how-scammers-turn-google-maps-into-fantasy-land xxv http://www.komonews.com/news/local/Man-used-Google-flaw-to-eavesdrop-on-calls-to-Secret-Service-FBI-247962881.html

xxvi http://www.sfbg.com/politics/2014/03/05/hacker-pranks-san-francisco-fbi-using-google-maps-exploit

xxvii http://en.wikipedia.org/wiki/Communications_Decency_Act

xxviii
http://commons.wikimedia.org/wiki/File:US_population_map.png by User: Jim Irwin

xxix http://en.wikipedia.org/wiki/HTTP_cookie

xxx https://support.google.com/business/answer/3038163?hl=en

Made in the USA
Middletown, DE
11 May 2016